# THE GERMAN
# HOME FRONT
## —1939-45—

# Terry Charman

# THE GERMAN HOME FRONT

## —1939-45—

Foreword by Martin Gilbert

PHILOSOPHICAL LIBRARY

*To Edward Szwed*

## ACKNOWLEDGEMENTS

I would like to thank all my friends and colleagues at the Imperial War Museum, London, and in particular those in the Departments of Art, Documents, Photographs and Printed Books: Ron Brooker, Colin Bruce, Jane Carmichael, Jane Fish, Anne Fleming, Toby Haggith, Robin Hamilton-Farey, Paul Kemp, Brad King, Michael Moody, Geoffrey O'Connor, David Parry, Philip Reed, Angela Weight, and Jenny Wood. Special thanks go to Pat Halpin, Lorine Lindsay, and Teresa Silk who typed the manuscript and captions, and to Martin Taylor for his constant help and encouragement. Thanks also to Tony Wells of the Wiener Library and Institute of Contemporary History, to Eileen Tweedy for the photography, to Andrew Shoolbred for the design, and to Sara Waterson for picture research. Finally, I would like to express my thanks to Paula Iley and Laurence King of John Calmann & King Ltd for their encouragement in the initial stages of work, and to Carolyn Yates, my editor, whose advice, assistance, encouragement, and occasional goading, has helped to make the writing of this book such a pleasure.

## PICTURE CREDITS

The author, the publishers, and John Calmann & King Ltd would like to thank the following for kindly allowing photographs to be reproduced in this book: Barnaby's Picture Library: pp. 53, 87; the British Film Institute: pp. 100, 101, 102, 167, 183; Novosti Press Agency: pp. 190, 197, 203, 210, 213, 217; Robert Hunt Library: cover, frontispiece, pp. 5, 6 (bottom), 7, 9 (top), 10 (bottom), 12 (bottom), 13 (top), 15, 17, 20, 22 (top & bottom right), 23, 26 (bottom), 27, 28 (top), 29 (top), 30 (right), 33, 34 (bottom, top left), 35, 36, 48 (right), 54–5, 71, 72 (top), 74–5, 76, 77 (top), 78, 79 (bottom), 80 (top), 81, 83, 92 (bottom), 93, 107, 109 (top right), 112, 120, 121 (bottom), 123 (bottom), 124 (top), 126 (bottom), 172, 173, 181, (bottom), 184 (bottom), 191, 214 (bottom), 220 (top,) 227; the Wiener Library: p. 90 (top); US Army: p. 205; the rest of the photographs appear by courtesy of the Imperial War Museum, London.

First published in the USA in 1989 by
Philosophical Library
31 West 21st Street, New York, NY 10010

© 1989 Terry Charman

Library of Congress Cataloging-in-Publication Data
Charman, T. C.
    The German Home Front, 1939–45/Terry
    Charman: introduction by Martin Gilbert.
    pp. 240    280 × 240 mm
    Includes index
    ISBN 0–8022–2568–3
    1. Germany–History–1933–1945.    2. World
    War, 1939–1945–Germany.
I. Title.
DD256.5.C547    1989        89–4044
943.086-dc20                CIP

This book was designed and produced by
JOHN CALMANN & KING LTD, LONDON

Designed by Andrew Shoolbred
Phototypset by Keyspools Ltd, UK
Printed in Spain by Cayfosa

*Girls from a Danzig school carrying the swastika banner on an excursion with their teacher in 1939.*
*"We want to make it clear what a girl's school today has to achieve. The subjects dealing with race and family, heredity, Germanism abroad and protection from air raids stand in the foreground of our whole instruction. In addition, swimming, cooking, the encouragement of music, domestic economy, and the whole of German history, all have to be mastered."*
*Ella Schubert, headmistress of a girl's school, in* Deutsches Frauenwerk, *January 1934.*

# Contents

# Foreword

Martin Gilbert

A great deal has been written about Hitler's victims. The geographic range of the Third Reich at the height of its powers was enormous; from the Arctic Circle to the Aegean Sea, and from the Atlantic Ocean to the Volga. Much less has been written about the German people themselves – both victims and perpetrators alike – during the years of Nazi rule. Yet even at the height of Germany's military victories, first in western Europe, then in the Balkans, and finally on the vast Eastern Front, many German people were under enormous pressures and strains.

Millions of them had thrilled to Hitler's victory in 1933, when, not as a result of an election, but amid a political crisis, he was invited to become Chancellor. For those millions, Germany was embarking upon an exciting experiment. The economy would flourish. New fast motor roads would criss-cross the land. Work would be found for all, and, in due course, Germany would be avenged on her enemies of the First World War.

Those who felt this way were excited and buoyed up by the torchlight procession on Hitler's first night of power, and by the many mass rallies that followed. But many of Germany's citizens were to be treated to all the harshness of a regime which had come to power with a fierce and formidable discipline.

Hitler had moved rapidly to establish his dictatorship. An Emergency Decree, passed by the Reichstag on 5 February 1933, expropriated all Communist Party buildings and printing presses, and closed down all pacifist organizations. In the following week, the stormtroops, encouraged by the enthusiasm of the constitutional victory, attacked trade union buildings, and beat up political opponents in the streets.

On 9 March 1933, the Stormtroops took to the streets of Berlin. This time, the principal victims were Jews. Many were beaten, the *Manchester Guardian* reported, "until the blood streamed down their heads and faces, and their backs and shoulders were bruised. Many fainted and were left lying on the streets ..." The Stormtroops worked in groups of between five and thirty men, "the whole gang often assaulting one person." Survivors were rounded up and sent to Dachau, the first of many concentration camps. Among fellow detainees were trade unionists, communists, liberals, opponents of the Nazi regime, humanitarians, homosexuals and gypsies.

From the very first days of Hitler's accession to power, creativity and destruction went hand in hand; exhilaration and fear were the twin emotions stalking Germany. The Nazi parades and songs and building programmes were the much-publicized positive side of the new regime. Arrest, incarceration, brutality, and death were its dark side, kept as secret as possible by the threat of reprisal, and the all-pervasive scrutiny of the Nazi Secret Police.

During those early months of Nazism's power, Hitler discovered that denouncing German Jews as the true enemy of the State won considerable popular support. Although many Germans were disgusted by the anti-Jewish denunciations and repelled by the anti-Jewish brutality, others followed Hitler's prejudice, and forgot whatever difficulties his regime imposed on them by concentrating their hostilities against the Jews. There followed the boycott of Jewish shops, the first of a string of moves designed to drive Jews firmly out of all walks of German society.

German Jews were stunned by this organized, absurd, cruel display, and within time half a million of them – many of whom had made important contributions to German science, medicine and culture, and had fought side by side with their fellow Germans in the trenches of the First World War – were driven slowly but inexorably out of German life. By giving German non-Jews the status of "Aryan," an imaginary concept, based upon nonsensical and discredited theories of "purity of race," Hitler formally divided German citizens into two groups. The very concept of "German Jewish" was further denied and denounced: one could either be a German, or one could be a Jew.

Despite frequent denunciations in the western European press, Hitler scorned foreign protest. At home, he used the police state, press censorship, arrest and torture to enhance his power. Abroad, he lulled his western European neighbors into a belief that his aims were peaceful, while secretly rearming. By 1937, his control of the German people was complete; he was free to turn his attentions elsewhere. "Greater Germany", which incorporated Austria, the Sudetenland, Bohemia and Moravia, now came into existence.

On 3 September 1939, three days after the invasion of Poland, both Britain and France declared war on Germany. Henceforth, Hitler's armies struck out more and more widely, attacking Denmark and Norway in April 1940, France, Belgium, Holland and Luxembourg in May 1940, Greece and Yugoslavia in April 1941, and the Soviet Union in June 1941. More and more nations, despite Hitler's first triumphs over them, were determined to defeat him and his regime. For many Germans, however, victory brought exhilaration and a sense of power, triumph and satisfaction.

In December 1941 Germany declared war on the United States,

then reeling under the blow of the Japanese attack on Pearl Harbor. But the German armies did not pose a serious threat to America. Indeed, it was now only a matter of time before the virtually limitless material resources of the United States and the manpower and military exertions of the Soviet Union would enable the Allies to defeat Germany.

For the German people, these pointers to defeat were not immediately evident. Vast numbers of forced laborers from all over Europe were at Germany's disposal. Several million Poles, Dutchmen, Frenchmen, Belgians and others were deported to Germany, to work in factories all over the Reich, and, when the Allied bombing began, to help clear the rubble. The forced labor system gave German industry and the German municipalities a substantial accretion of manpower at the very moment when more and more able-bodied men were being sent to the war fronts.

The bombing power of the Allies was also slow to manifest itself. In 1940 and 1941, it was German bombers which wreaked havoc elsewhere: on Warsaw, Rotterdam, Coventry, London, Belgrade and on the cities of the Soviet Union. But, at first on a small scale, then with larger and larger raids and heavier and heavier bombs, the Allies, and in particular the Anglo-American air forces, brought fire and destruction to almost every German city, on a scale which, by 1943, far outweighed anything the German air force had been able to inflict. The death of 40,000 citizens in Hamburg in a few hours during an air raid in 1942 was awful proof of the power of retaliation.

The people of Germany were beginning to feel the weight of military power which earlier they had imposed on a dozen nations. First bombs from the air, and then armies across the land, destroyed the Nazi vision and its perverse evils but not before Nazism had continued its ruthless purging of the nation, seeking out all those born with mental defects. From the first weeks of the war, a euthanasia programme directed from Hitler's Chancellery accounted for the murder by gas and injection of more than 150,000 Germans judged "unfit to live." Thousands of German homosexuals and gypsies were likewise murdered; Jewish persecution continued until the end, with victims numbering some 250,000 in Germany itself and six million in other European states. Moreover, in an attempt to "purify" the whole of Europe, three million Poles and one million Serbs were also murdered in cold blood. A further three and a half million Russian prisoners-of-war were killed or starved to death after they had been captured.

With enormous courage, many thousands of Germans tried to oppose these cruel manifestations of the regime for which many of them had voted a decade earlier. Thousands of German patriots, for example, were put to death after the failure of the bomb plot against Hitler in July 1944. In the final months of war, the execution of German opponents to Nazism accelerated, even as the Allied armies were advancing on Berlin.

The promise of creativity and construction, which in 1933 had attracted so many Germans, had given way to mass destruction of human life. When, on 25 April 1945, American and Soviet forces met at the village of Torgau on the River Elbe, much of Germany was in ruins. Great cities like Hamburg and Dresden, and Berlin itself, had been reduced to ruins, and the German people, who a mere three years earlier had held so much of Europe in thrall, were now themselves conquered and their country partitioned.

Nor was it a matter only of defeat. In numerical terms the German people, who in September 1939, in May 1940, and in April and June 1941, envisaged only short wars and swift victories over the countries they attacked — in each case without warning or declaration of war — took a heavy toll: about 3,600,000 German civilians were killed in more than two years of intense air bombardment, and a further 3,250,000 German soldiers were killed in action, mostly on the Eastern Front — a total death toll of 6,850,000, more than one in ten of all Germans. In 1933 Hitler promised triumph and victory: by 1945, he had achieved the decimation of the German people.

*Merton College, Oxford*
13 April 1989

# 1933–1939

28 June 1933: The fourteenth anniversary of the signing of the Treaty of Versailles provokes a Nazi-orchestrated demonstration against it on the Wilhelmplatz in Berlin.

# "Signs of a new era"

From his Berlin headquarters at the Kaiserhof Hotel Adolf Hitler crossed the Wilhelmstrasse at noon on 30 January 1933 to receive from President Paul von Hindenburg his nomination as Chancellor of the Reich. That night Paul Joseph Goebbels wrote in his diary:

> It seems like a dream. The Wilhelmstrasse is ours. The Leader is already working in Chancellery. We stand in the window upstairs, watching hundreds and thousands of young people march past the aged President of the Reich and the young Chancellor in the flaming torchlight, shouting their joy and gratitude.

Cynics claimed that the aged and senile president, a First World War hero, turned to an aide and asked of the marchers "Did we really take all these Russians prisoners at Tannenberg?" But a Jewish newspaperwoman saw it as "... an ominous night. A night of deadly menace, a nightmare in the living reality of 20,000 blazing torches." To all however, it was obvious that, in Goebbels' words, "The German Revolution has begun!"

Barely a month after the nomination of Hitler as Chancellor, the Reichstag building was set alight, most probably by a demented young Dutch Communist, Marinus van der Lubbe. The fire however gave the Nazis the green light to act against the German Communist Party just before the last multi-party Reichstag election on 5 March 1933, in which the Nazis, despite their apparatus of terror, still only won 44 per cent of the vote (288 seats).

Three weeks later the Enabling Law was passed giving Hitler almost complete dictatorial powers; only the Social Democrats voted against the law. The Nazification of German life now began apace. On 1 April 1933 there was the boycott of Jewish shops; a month later (2 May 1933) trade unions were banned, and on 10 May the first book burning took place at the University of Berlin. A Reich Chamber of Culture was established on 22 September to supervise all aspects of German cultural life. On 20 July the regime gained kudos abroad by signing a concordat with the Vatican; three months later however, on 19 October, Hitler withdrew Germany from the League of Nations. Some eight months later he felt strong enough to deal with those members of his party who believed that the Nazi revolution had not gone far enough, those calling for a second social revolution. Thus, on 30 June 1934, the "Night of the Long Knives," Hitler purged the leadership of the SA (*Sturmabteilungen*) including its chief of staff, Ernst Roehm. Other past opponents including a former chancellor, General Kurt von Schleicher, and former Nazi Party chieftain Gregor Strasser were also liquidated. "At that hour," proclaimed Hitler in the

*A cigarette card in the series* Das Neue Reich *(the New Reich) showing the trial of Marinus van der Lubbe after the Reichstag fire.*

On 1 April 1933 the first boycott of Jewish shops, lawyers and doctors took place all over Germany. Members of the SA and SS stood outside Jewish stores and reminded each would-be shopper of the boycott slogan: ''Germans protect yourselves. Do not buy from Jews.''

The Olympic Stadium packed with a crowd of 120,000 to hear Goebbels give a speech on the occasion of the Summer Solstice 1939. Immediately after the Berlin Olympics of 1936 Hitler instructed Albert Speer to prepare plans for a new stadium that would hold 400,000. When told that such a vast structure would meet neither the specifications of the International Olympic Committee nor the requirements of conventional athletics, Hitler replied: ''In 1940 the Olympic Games will take place in Tokyo. But thereafter they will take place in Germany for all time to come, in this stadium. And then we will determine the measurements of the athletic field.''

*(Right)  On 10 May 1933 students at the University of Berlin collected from both private and public libraries some 20,000 ''un-German books'' for a public book-burning on the Franz Josef Platz in the presence of Goebbels and other notabilities. Into the flames were consigned the works of German authors such as Thomas and Heinrich Mann, Lion Feuchtwanger, Erich Maria Remarque, Ernst Toller, Arnold Zweig, and foreigners, H. G. Wells, Jack London, André Gide, Emile Zola and Marcel Proust.*

*(Below)  Book-burning at the University of Berlin.*

Reichstag, "I was responsible for the fate of the German nation and the supreme judge of the German nation." Barely a month later, on 2 August, Hindenburg died and Hitler, doing away with the office of President, proclaimed his own succession as Führer and Chancellor. The army, grateful for the purging of the SA, generally considered its potential rival, took a personal oath of allegiance to Hitler the following day.

On 19 August 1934 Hitler held a plebiscite to confirm his assumption of the role of head of state as well as government. This was the second plebiscite of the Nazi regime, the first having been held in the previous year following the decision to leave the League of Nations. Thirty-eight million Germans voted their approval of the Führer's action. The next month the Nazi Party Congress took place as usual at Nuremberg under the slogan *Parteitag der Treue* (Party Congress of Loyalty). It was filmed by Leni Riefenstahl, Hitler's favorite film producer, as *Triumph des Willens* (Triumph of the Will). At the congress, military units of the Army and Navy took part in the celebrations for the first time, thus confirming and emphasizing the unity of Party and State. Fresh triumphs came early in 1935.

On 13 January the Saar plebiscite took place. By a massive majority—477,000 to 48,000—the inhabitants of the Saar voted to return their coal-rich territory to Germany, and Hitler publicly proclaimed that Germany now had no further territorial claims on France. Two months later on 16 March the Führer reinstated general conscription in open violation of the Treaty of Versailles. The action was popular in Germany where the ban on a conscript army was considered a national humiliation. The same day it was officially acknowledged that an air force (Luftwaffe) was in existence with Hermann Goering at its helm as commander-in-chief. The Party Congress in 1935, ironically, the Party Congress of Freedom, was marked by further measures against the Jews. Its outcome, the so-called Nuremberg Laws explicitly deprived Jews of the rights of full German citizenship, placed a ban on mixed marriages between Jews and "Aryans," and forbade Jews to employ female domestics of "Aryan" origin. The swastika banner was also formally adopted as the German national flag.

On 7 March 1936, against the advice of his generals, Hitler ordered German troops to march into the Rhineland, which had been "demilitarized" under the terms of the Treaty of Versailles. This action was accompanied by a repudiation of the Locarno Treaty under the pretext that it had already been violated by the recently-concluded agreement between France and Russia. The same day Hitler dissolved the Reichstag and called for a new election and referendum on his Rhineland "coup." According to the official voting figures on 29 March some 99 per cent of the 45,454,691 registered voters went to the polling booths, and 98.8 per cent of them approved the Führer's action. The new Zeppelin *Hindenburg* was used by Goebbels, Minister of Propaganda and Public Enlightenment since 13 March 1933, to cruise over German cities as a publicity stunt as the poll took place. Forty-two people voted "Ja," boasted the Minister on the Zeppelin, a statistic that outnumbered the total number of persons aboard by two! Foreign observers, however, had no doubt that the majority of Germans did support the reoccupation of the Rhineland and the defiance of the detested Versailles *Diktat*.

*Hitler's* Mein Kampf *and Nazi Party philosopher Alfred Rosenberg's* Myth of the Twentieth Century *on sale in occupied Prague.*
*"The National Church of the German Reich declares that the greatest written document of our people is the book of our Führer,* Mein Kampf. *It is completely aware that this book incorporates not only the greatest but also the purest and truest ethics for the present life of our people."*
*Paragraph XVI, programme of thirty points of the National Church of the German Reich, quoted in the* Manchester Guardian, *6 May 1936.*

(Right) With the death of Hindenburg on 2 August 1934 the Reich's armed forces had a new oath of allegiance to swear: "I swear by God this holy oath, that I will render to Adolf Hitler, Leader of the German nation and people, Supreme Commander of the Armed Forces, unconditional obedience, and I am ready as a brave soldier to risk my life at any time for this oath."

(Below) On 13 January 1935 the people of the Saar voted in a plebiscite, policed by British, Italian, Dutch and Swedish troops, to return to the Reich by a majority of 477,000 to 48,000. Here young girls are making victory garlands to decorate the streets before the Führer's arrival on 1 March.

Further prestige came to the regime in August 1936 when Germany hosted the Eleventh Olympic Games. The Nazis saw this occasion as a great opportunity to impress foreign visitors with the achievements of the Third Reich. Infinite trouble was taken with the training of German athletes, who would show the world what Hitler's Germany could accomplish in the field of sport (German athletes came top in the medals tables with 33 gold, 26 silver and 30 bronze, to the USA's 24, 20, and 12) and vast sums were spent on projects to entertain foreign visitors. An Olympic Village, magnificently equipped, was built near Berlin to house the foreign competitors. A sports stadium, the *Reichssportsfeld*, was erected, which was intended to surpass in resplendence all other sports stadiums in the world. An open theater was specially constructed, in which Germany's foremost actors and singers

*An aerial view of the Olympic Stadium at the* Reichssportsfeld *taken during the XI Olympics, August 1936. The stadium held capacity crowds of 110,000 almost every afternoon during the field and track events when black American athlete Jesse Owens' victories made a mockery of Nazi racial theories. Hitler later refused to shake his hand at the medals ceremony.*

*A pre-*Anschluss *referendum poster.*

gave performances throughout the period of the Games. The Nazi leaders, particularly Goebbels and Goering, vied with each other in party-giving and entertaining prominent foreign guests. For the duration of the Games the persecution of the Roman Catholic and Protestant Churches was soft-pedalled, and signs proclaiming "Juden unerwünscht" (Jews not wanted) were taken down. The same month the period of compulsory military service was fixed at two years.

After the undoubted success of the Olympics the Nazi Party Congress of Honor was held the following month and resulted in the proclamation of the Second Four Years' Plan. The goal of the first Four Years' Plan had been the abolition of unemployment, a goal which had now been virtually attained (mainly through the effects of conscription, rearmament and "directed" labor). The purpose of the second plan was, according to Hitler, "to make Germany independent of foreign countries for all those materials which can possibly be manufactured in Germany."

Goering was made responsible for the execution of the plan, and with his customary bluff forthrightness, made it clear in his speeches that the Second Four Years' Plan had been conceived with a view to building up German military strength. Faced, he said, with the choice between "guns and butter," the German people would unhesitatingly choose guns. The same year saw the appointment of Himmler as Chief of the German Police (16 June 1936) and the institution also in June of the block system in the Nazi Party; a system which ensured the close control of each individual from the standpoint of his "political reliability." As the year was coming to a close, it was announced on 1 December that henceforth all German boys and girls must join the *Hitlerjugend* (Hitler Youth) and the *Bund deutscher Mädel* (League of German Maidens).

*(Right) Nazi electioneering in pre-*Anschluss *Vienna: among the targets on the billboard are the Roman Catholic Church, Freemasons, "Bolsheviks" and the "lying Jewish press." The slogan above the Stormtrooper trumpeters reads "Vienna awake!" (the Nazi slogan in Germany before 30 January 1933 having been "Germany awake!").*

*(Left) "Jews are not wanted here" reads this banner in the village of Rosenheim, Bavaria. Other towns had similar signs "Jews strictly forbidden in this town," "Jews enter at their own risk." And at Ludwigshafen at a bend in the road a sign was put up: "Drive carefully! Sharp curve! Jews 120 km an hour!"*

(Right) In defiance of the Treaty of Versailles German troops reoccupy the demilitarized zone of the Rhineland on 7 March 1936. ''The forty-eight hours after the march into the Rhineland were the most nerve-racking in my life. If the French had then marched . . . we would have had to withdraw with our tails between our legs, for the military resources at our disposal would have been wholly inadequate for even a moderate resistance,'' Hitler was to say later.

(Below) Between seven and eight o'clock on the morning of Saturday 12 March 1938 the first units of the Wehrmacht crossed the Austro-German border. Here mounted troops are seen in Salzburg. Many German motorized and armored units broke down during the Austrian Blumenkrieg (''flower-war''—after the gifts of flowers given to the troops by welcoming crowds).

1937, known as the "Year of No Surprises," began with the fourth anniversary of the accession to power on 30 January, when Hitler addressed a special meeting of the Reichstag, and reviewed the social achievements of the regime, emphasizing the reduction by five million in the numbers of unemployed since January 1933. In May 1937, the ban on new members of the Nazi Party, imposed in April 1933, was relaxed, and at the Party Congress of Labor at Nuremberg that September Hitler declared that the Treaty of Versailles was dead.

1938 began with the removal, from both armed forces and government, of top men thought to be less than enthusiastic about the Führer's plans for aggressive expansion. The War Minister, Field-Marshal Werner von Blomberg, for instance, resigned over a scandal involving his second wife, "a woman of lowly origin and reputedly doubtful virtue." At the same time Army commander-in-chief General Werner von Fritsch was forced out, the victim of a smear campaign masterminded by Himmler's deputy Reinhard Heydrich. Hitler announced that he himself was assuming the supreme command of the armed forces, and the post of Minister of War was abolished. At the Foreign Office Konstantin von Neurath was replaced by Joachim von Ribbentrop, the ex-ambassador to Britain, of whom Mussolini once said: "You only have to look at his head to see what a small brain he has." The stage was now set for foreign "adventures."

On 12 March German troops marched into Austria followed by the Führer who proclaimed the *Anschluss* (union) of his homeland with Germany. A plebiscite (the last during the Third Reich) was held in April, and 99.08 per cent of Germans voted in favor of the *Anschluss*. This figure is, however, nowadays often disputed, considered by many a gross exaggeration for propaganda purposes. Throughout the summer of 1938 pressure was brought to bear on Czechoslovakia, the consequence of which was the annexation of the Sudetenland in October following the four

*Members of the BDM (*Bund deutscher Mädel, *the League of German Maidens) report to a Berlin industrial training establishment to "do their bit" on the home front, 1939. "... then the girls must be educated as Spartans in the labor service. They must be accustomed to the palliasse, to renouncing all cosmetics, to wearing simple dress that makes individual coquettishness impossible, in order to be wholly hardened". Quoted in* Berliner Tageblatt, *8 January 1936.*

(Left) Hitler being greeted on the balcony of his hotel in Karlsbad during the annexation of the Sudetenland, 3 October 1938.

(Right) A page from a Nazi nursery school book. The verse is the first of the Horst Wessel Lied, the Nazi party anthem.

(Below) Sudeten-German women greet the occupying Wehrmacht troops in October 1938.

Die Fahne hoch! Die Reihen dicht geschlossen,
S.A. marschiert mit mutig festem Schritt.
Kam'raden, die Rotfront und Reaktion erschossen,
Marschier'n im Geist in unsern Reihen mit.

(Left) 3 October 1938: the townsfolk of Eger, many of them dressed in traditional local German costume such as these girls here, give Hitler a rapturous welcome.

(Above) Wildly enthusiastic crowds greet Hitler during his triumphant entry into Eger in the Sudetenland where Konrad Henlein, the leader of the Sudeten-German Party, hailed him as "a liberator."

*(Right) Sunbathers and swimmers relaxing at the Wannsee, Berlin. In the summer of 1942 Himmler decreed that bathing in the nude was now permissible again. The Nazis had ceremoniously forbidden it in 1933 on the grounds that it was a symptom of the general moral decline under the Weimar Republic.*

*Some of the first* Volkswagen *(KdF-Wagen)—parked under an Autobahn bridge—are shown off to foreign press correspondents.*
*''We hope the KdF car will even raise the German birth-rate by encouraging German families to have four or five children to fill it.''*
*Dr Robert Ley, 15 August 1938.*

power Munich Conference, (29–30 September 1938), the greatest triumph, superficially, of Hitler's foreign policy by blackmail.

Earlier that year, in May, before the Czech crisis had loomed, Hitler had laid the foundation stone of the German People's Car Factory at Fallersleben, in Lower Saxony. The People's Car (*Volkswagen*) was to cost 990 marks (248 dollars) and was sold on an instalment basis, with people contributing so much per month over an established period of time before finally receiving their car. Many people subscribed enthusiastically; no cars were ever delivered. As far back as 20 August 1933 Hitler had given orders for the construction of *Reichsautostrassen* (auto highways) throughout the Reich. By September 1936 it was announced that the first 1,000 kilometers of those motorways, now renamed *Autobahnen*, had been completed. As foreign observers noted, the peacetime traffic did not justify the building of these motor highways, but there was little doubt as to the value they would have in time of war. The *Volkswagen* scheme was one of the responsibilities of the *Deutsche Arbeitsfront* (German Labor Front) headed by Dr Robert Ley, whose weakness for the bottle caused endless complications throughout his career.

*A page from an anti-Semitic school book for primary school children purporting to show the immorality of Jews.*

*Anti-Semitic slogans painted on the wall of a Jewish shop following Kristallnacht, supposedly a ''manifestation of popular indignation'' against the Jews, but in reality a carefully and officially prepared pogrom. Orders received by an SA group in Mannheim read: ''By the orders of the group leader, all Jewish synagogues within the territory of Brigade 50 are to be blown up or set on fire immediately. Neighboring houses inhabited by Aryans must not be damaged. This action is to be carried out in civilian clothes. Riots and looting are to be prevented. You are to report the completion of your assignment to headquarters or the brigade leader at any time before 8.30 am.''*

WUCHER UND HEHLEREI
WAREN VON JEHER IHR PRIVILEG

VOR RASSENSCHANDE
WARNTE DIE JUDENTRACHT

*Nazi officials at an anti-Semitic exhibition, 1938.*

The *Deutsche Arbeitsfront* was a mixed body of employers and employees, and was designed to replace the banned trade unions. A sub-section of the DAF was the *Kraft durch Freude* (Strength through Joy) movement, which was responsible for the provision of entertainment and recreational facilities for German workers. These ranged from factory concerts to cruises on the ships of the *Kraft durch Freude* fleet to Madeira and the Norwegian fjords.

Relief amongst the German people was heartfelt when the Sudeten crisis was settled peacefully at the Munich Conference, but the following month an event occurred which both blackened Germany's name abroad and caused deep shock and shame to many Germans at home. On 7 November, a young Polish Jew named Herschel Grynszpan, an unemployed seventeen-year-old, shot and killed the Third Secretary of the German Embassy in Paris, Ernst vom Rath. He did it, Grynszpan declared, to avenge Nazi treatment of his fellow Jews. The death of vom Rath, ironically an anti-Nazi who was undergoing investigation and surveillance by Himmler's men at the time of his death, was made the excuse for a nationwide action

*German expansion 1933–39.*

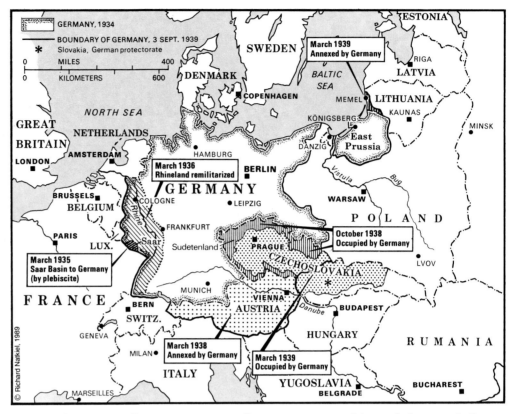

against the Jews still in Germany. A ''spontaneous uprising of the people'' was organized for November 9 and 10, which resulted in the wrecking of 7,500 Jewish shops and 119 synagogues and in the deaths of 35 Jews. Thousands more were arrested and sent to the concentration camps, which had been a feature of German life since March 1933. So many shop windows were smashed—to the tune of five million marks ($1,250,000)—that the ''spontaneous uprising'' became known as *Kristallnacht* (Crystal Night or Night of Broken Glass). Public opinion throughout the world was horrified at this pogrom, and President Roosevelt withdrew the American Ambassador, Hugh Wilson, ''to report.''

1939 was almost completely dominated by events abroad which were to lead to the outbreak of war. On January 30 Hitler gave notice of his intention to exterminate European Jewry when he stated:

> If the international Jewish financiers . . . should succeed again in plunging the nations into a world war, the result will be . . . the annihilation of the Jewish race throughout Europe.

He was to repeat this prophecy five times verbatim, in subsequent public utterances over the next four years. It was to fall on deaf ears. Yet enormous queues of German Jews were to be found at the consulates of those nations likely to allow immigration although roughly half the Jewish population (about 250,000 people) had emigrated since 1933. For later emigrants the fate of those aboard the liner *St. Louis* in the early summer of 1939, who were denied entry into Cuba and were only taken on sufferance by Britain, France, Holland and Belgium, was not a very hopeful augury. Of the remaining Jews, only a few thousand were to survive the war.

(Right) "Danzig greets its Führer!" reads the banner above Hitler as he rides into the beflagged former Free City to make a triumphal speech at the Artushof.

(Below) Men of the Danzig Heimwehr (Home Army) on manoeuvers outside the Free City shortly before the war.

*(From left) A token from the* Kreis *of Tecklenburg; a Youth Festival badge, 1937; a token bearing the Führer's head from Gau Westfalen Nord; and a badge commemorating May Day, the day of the workers.*

Hitler's next move was to occupy the Czech provinces of Bohemia-Moravia in defiance of the Munich Agreement and to take Slovakia into "protection" on 15 March 1939; a week later, on 23 March, he instigated the reoccupation of the Baltic part of Memel which had been occupied by Lithuania since 1921. This was to be the last of the Führer's bloodless conquests.

Throughout the summer of 1939 German propaganda concentrated on the villainies of the Poles in their treatment of the German minority in the so-called Polish Corridor, and on the position of the Free City of Danzig with its overwhelmingly German population who wanted to "return to the Reich." The orchestrated press and radio fed the German people a steady diet of fabricated "atrocities:" "Complete chaos in Poland—German families flee—Polish soldiers push to edge of German border" were the headlines of the *Berliner Börsen Zeitung* on 26 August 1939, while on the same day the afternoon paper *12-Uhr Blatt* claimed: "This playing with fire going too far—three German passenger planes shot at by Poles—In Corridor many German farmhouses in flames."

To provide a pretext for the attack on Poland, a simulated raid on the radio transmitter at Gleiwitz in Silesia was made by SS men under the command of Alfred Naujocks on the night of 31 August 1939. Clad in Polish uniforms, Naujocks and his men broke into the radio station, where one of the raiders delivered an inflammatory speech in Polish:

> People of Poland: The time has come for war between Poland and Germany!
> Unite and smash down any German, all Germans who oppose your war.
> Trample all resistance! The time has come!

*(Left) On 1 December 1936 a new law was passed regarding the Hitler Youth. Article 2 stated: "In addition to the training received at home and school, all German young people are to become members of the Hitler Youth in order to receive a physical, mental and moral education in the spirit of National Socialism that will enable them to serve their people and the nation as a whole." The photograph shows Hitler Youths from Vienna at their summer camp on the Wörthersee.*

After firing a few shots the raiders withdrew, leaving behind them the blood-soaked bodies of drugged concentration camp prisoners in Polish uniforms who had been promised their freedom for allegedly taking part in a film. The underhand operation was given the cynical codename "Canned Goods" and provided Hitler with the opportunity to declare in the Reichstag the next day that there had been an "attack by regular Polish troops on the Gleiwitz transmitter." He went on to say:

> In order to put an end to this lunacy, I have no other choice than to meet
> force with force from now on.

The opening of hostilities had been announced on the radio earlier that morning. World War Two had begun.

(Above)  A pre-war Nazi election poster aimed at farmers: ''We farmers are mucking out'' reads the slogan, as the Aryan farmer-figure clears away the capitalist, the Bolshevik, the pressman, and the Jew.

(Above, right)  Goebbels and his daughter Helga with Hitler at the Berghof. Helga, born on 1 September 1932, was poisoned by her parents—along with her four sisters and brother—in the Führerbunker on 1 May 1945.

(Right)  A night at the opera. The Nazi élite at a performance of the Meistersingers of Nuremberg at the Charlottenburg Opera on 16 November 1935. From right: Goebbels, Frau Hess, Hitler, Frau Goebbels, Frau Goering and Goering.

(Opposite)  The 550th anniversary of the founding of Germany's oldest university, celebrated by representatives from 31 countries in a parade, led by the professors, through the beflagged streets of Heidelberg.

(Opposite) A pre-war photograph of Hitler being presented with a bouquet by a young admirer.

(Below) Thomas Mann, banned author and one of the earliest emigrés from the Third Reich, broadcast to his countrymen during the war in programmes that went out on the BBC's German Service. Here a cartoon from Streicher's Der Stürmer shows Mann, spokesman for the New York Jews, giving aid to England, 21 November 1940.

(Above) German Christian students holding a meeting in the Opernplatz in Berlin
"To us now is risen the incarnation of what Christianity really is: Adolf Hitler."
Hans Kerrl, Reich Minister for Church Affairs, 13 February 1937.

(Above, right) A pre-war election poster bearing the slogan "Our last hope: Hitler."

(Right) A mother and her garlanded daughter wave to passing Party officials.

*(Right)  On 22 February 1933 Goering established an auxiliary police force of 50,000 men, of whom 40,000 came from the SS and SA, to combat "those hostile to the State." Goering said in a speech at Dortmund: "Whoever does his duty in the service of the state, who obeys my orders and ruthlessly makes use of his revolver when attacked is assured of my protection . . . a bullet fired from the barrel of a police gun is my bullet. If you say that is murder, then I am the murderer." Here suspects are arrested by auxiliary policemen in 1933.*

*(Below)  Girls of the* Bund deutscher Mädel *(League of German Maidens) at a pre-war rally.*

(Above)  A group of Hitler Youths at table in a hostel decorated in folkloristic style.

(Right)  Two members of the Wehrmacht demonstrate the working of a heavy machine gun to a group of Jungvolk. One boy described such a session in a letter: "... throwing the grenades was rather tiring but it kept us amused. The lesson lasted an hour. We were given wooden imitations of hand grenades weighing 800 grammes. We were told just how to handle them and how best to throw them from all positions."

(Above) A pre-war poster calling on the youth of Germany to join a march to Nuremberg.

(Right) At a pre-war Nuremberg Rally members of the Hitler Youth applaud the Führer.
"The youth . . . will terrify the world. I want a youth that is violent, masterful, intrepid, cruel. Young people must be all these things. They must endure pain."
Adolf Hitler, 1937.

*(Right) Swimmers taking physical exercise at Wannsee's open-air swimming pool. The instructor's megaphone comes from the Sports Office of the Berlin section of the "Strength through Joy" organization. Great emphasis was placed on physical fitness.*

*A leisure resort just outside Vienna. Swedish correspondent Arvid Fredborg on a visit to the Austrian capital in February 1943 noted that "the food seemed almost Elysian to one who came from Berlin. Palatschinken, thin pancakes, were still being served at the old aristocratic Sacher restaurant, and their quality had not deteriorated. The soups were delicious and contained no chemicals, and the bread was considerably better than in the German capital."*

(Above) *A banner calling for a "yes"
vote in the plebiscite of 10 April 1938
concerning the reunion of Austria with the
Reich. According to official figures,
99.08% of the population in Germany
and 99.75% of the population in Austria
voted for the Anschluss.*

(Below) *"Two German women in tears
at the thought of meeting and shaking
hands with Hitler," was the original
caption to this photograph.
"In the education of women emphasis
must be laid primarily on physical
development. Only afterwards must
consideration be given to the spiritual
values, and lastly to mental
development."* Adolf Hitler.

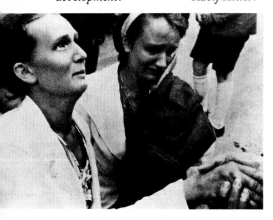

*(Opposite) Vienna, 10 March 1938 and supporters of Austrian "Bundeskanzler" Dr Kurt von Schuschnigg campaign for votes. Four days later Hitler made his triumphant entry into the city, after Himmler had arrested some 67,000 Austrians "for reasons of security."*

*(Right) A "Strength through Joy" holiday cruise to Madeira, which cost only $25, including the rail fare to and from the German port. Special winter excursions were also organized at a cost of $11 a week, which included the fare, room and board, rental of skis and lessons from a ski instructor.*

*(Right) The burned-out wreck of "Strength through Joy" liner, Robert Ley, custom-built for taking German workers on pleasure cruises to Madeira, the Norwegian Fjords and the Mediterranean. During the war the Robert Ley was converted into a hospital/depot ship and assisted in the evacuation of Germans from East Prussia. Its sister ship the Wilhelm Gustloff was sunk with heavy loss of life on the night of 30 January 1945.*

(Right) The opening of the 1939–40 Winter Relief Fund in Berlin, 10 October 1939. In his speech that day Hitler declared: "We want to give each individual an insight into the real misery of many of the people. Every individual must realize that fortune and wealth have not come to all of us, nor will they. There has always been misery; there is misery today; there will always be misery." The campaign is opened with music and collecting on the streets.

(Below) A peaceful scene in a Hamburg beergarden, 1938. The Allied attacks on the city, Germany's principal port, in July 1943 left the city devastated, 30,000 dead, and 800,000 homeless.

(Above) Citizens of Prague examine a
recruiting poster for the Allgemeine
(General) SS. By the end of the war the
SS fighting branch, the Waffen SS,
numbered 900,000 many of whom were
non-Germans.

(Below) Motorized units of the
Wehrmacht enter the Czech capital,
greeted enthusiastically by a few
German residents with the Nazi salute.
From others the welcome was more
muted.

(Above) Saturday 12 March 1938:
Hitler returns to his "home town" Linz.

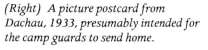

*(Right)* A picture postcard from Dachau, 1933, presumably intended for the camp guards to send home.

*(Below)* Prisoners at work in Dachau concentration camp, near Munich. Dachau was the first concentration camp to be set up, originally to hold Social Demcorats and Communists, on 22 March 1933.

LAGER DACHAU

Originalphoto der SS von Dachau 1933

*(Right)* An early anti-Nazi cartoon playing upon the Nazi ideal of motherhood: *"Fascism is War"* reads the inscription above the Hitler *"death's head."*

*(Far right)* An extract from a Jungvolk song and poetry book, which includes a pledge of loyalty to *"Mein Führer."* Here, Hitler's role is that of a third parent—to whom a child should promise love, obedience, help, and joy.

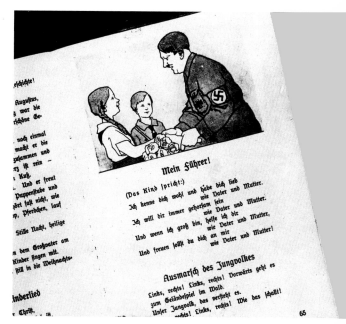

*Hitler Youths in Berlin at a pre-war fund-raising rally.*

35

*Peasants folk-dancing in traditional costume. Ruth Andreas-Friedrich noted in her diary on 30 August 1943 that to the peasants ''city dwellers are of no interest unless they barter goods. Safety from bombing they regard as a personal favour to us. . . . They trade bacon for dress goods, eggs for jewellery, butter for silk stockings.''*

*Goering distributing portraits of Hitler at a pre-war charity ball.*

*Two* Jungvolk *at a pre-war rally.*

# 1939–1940

*A group of cheerful evacuees waving swastika flags leave Vienna for the safety of the countryside. The first major evacuation scheme took place in September 1939 and mostly affected Germany's western areas, 500,000 people being moved from the Saar-Pfalz. The sick and infirm, the elderly and children under the age of ten were the first to be evacuated.*

# "These years of triumph"

*(Opposite) "The enemy sees your light! Black out!" reads this dramatic poster, produced by the German Propaganda Studio (DPA), and commissioned by the Propaganda Ministry. The improper use of flashlights during the blackout could lead to arrest and a fifty-mark ($25) fine.*

*A cigarette card from the* Das Neue Reich *series showing a Nuremberg rally.*

In August 1914 when Britain had declared war on Germany English residents were subjected to a variety of indignities, and the British Embassy building was attacked by a howling mob. Extreme chauvinism was the order of the day with Kaiser Wilhelm II proclaiming: "I know no parties any more. Only Germans." Twenty-five years later things were very different. Hitler's speech to the Reichstag on 1 September 1939 was listened to in resignation rather than exultation:

> No one cheered at the end of his speech, not even my aunt who had always cheered for Hitler; no one cried "Heil!" or turned somersaults with joy.
>
> Perturbation was written on everyone's face. No one spoke, and even the neighbors who had come to listen with us said nothing,

recalled Max von der Grun, then a thirteen-year-old boy living in the Fichtelgebirge region on the Czech border. Two days later in the capital, William L. Shirer, radio correspondent for the Columbia Broadcasting System, found barely 250 people in the Wilhelmstrasse as news of the British declaration came through. He noted how the crowd listened attentively to the announcement at 1.22 pm and their silence when it was over. Soon newspaperboys appeared with extras of the Berlin leading daily *Deutsche Allgemeine Zeitung* which were given away free of charge. The headlines read:

BRITISH ULTIMATUM TURNED DOWN

ENGLAND DECLARES A STATE OF WAR WITH GERMANY

BRITISH NOTE DEMANDS WITHDRAWAL OF OUR TROOPS IN THE EAST

THE FÜHRER LEAVING TODAY FOR THE FRONT

GERMAN MEMORANDUM PROVES ENGLAND'S GUILT

Outside the British Embassy "a lone *Schupo* [policeman] paced up and down before the building. He had nothing to do but saunter back and forth." John McCutcheon Raleigh of the *Chicago Tribune* observed the public's reaction to the news, noting that Berliners on their usual Sunday constitutional were unsmiling, murmuring their astonishment at the terrible thing that had happened. "Shoulders slumped. Steps were slow. Faces were long."

Already Berlin was taking on the look of a city at war. The blackout, (*Verdunklung*) had begun at 8 pm sharp on Friday 1 September. Earlier, in August, the capital and other cities throughout Germany had experimented with practice blackouts lasting several nights, but this was the real thing and there was a genuine fear that the Poles would launch an air attack on Berlin. Indeed, on the night of Saturday 2 September the sirens wailed, and a rumor circulated that 70 Polish bombers were on their way to the capital. This rumor, like so many in wartime,

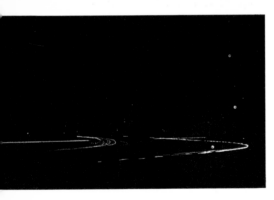

*(Above)  A series of photographs showing the effectiveness of the blackout around the Kaiser Wilhelm Memorial Church in Berlin.*

*(Right)  Hitler Youths paint white lines on a city street to enable pedestrians to find their way in the blackout.*

proved groundless. The hapless Poles were in no position to launch such an attack, and when Britain declared war, apart from one ineffectual attack on the German Fleet at Wilhelmshaven, the Royal Air Force confined its activities to dropping propaganda leaflets, in an attempt, as Churchill put it, ''to rouse the Germans to a higher morality.'' Despite the propaganda campaign against the Poles there were no signs of xenophobia as had been seen in 1914. Wallace Deuel of the *Chicago Daily News* reported:

> A car with a diplomatic licence, piled high inside with clothes and rugs, stopped at an intersection, and a man called out from the pavement, ''You'd better get out of here.'' But nobody paid any attention either to the man or the car. A few feet away a fat, berouged and painfully corseted woman of 50 did not even take her greedy eyes off a new model evening gown in a shop window to see what was happening.

In most cities and towns kerbs and street-crossings were painted luminous white, and cellar gratings everywhere covered with bulky sandbags, streaked with white paint. Flashlights became scarce as reserve stocks had been sold out weeks before the war in anticipation of the blackout. For those in possession of a flashlight, special regulations stipulated that bulbs had to be dark blue, or bulb casings covered with black or red paper. It seemed that practically every German wore a phosphorus button on his or her coat, so that ''thousands of small buttons glowed and bobbed along the Kurfürstendamm each night.'' Enthusiastic Nazi Party members wore phosphorus buttons in the shape of the swastika.

U.S. Embassy clerk William Russell noticed that the blackout had a strange effect on people: ''They all talk in whispers and low voices as they walk along the dark

streets, almost as if they fear the enemy could overhear them and drop some bombs down on them." Wallace Deuel described the blackout street scene:

> Buses ran with only single, ghoulish blue lights. Tram cars had faint illumination on their route numbers, but inside all the lights were shrouded in black cloth hoods. Motor car headlights were blackened except for narrow slits. A faint square of paleness glowed here and there through darkening material that was not quite opaque on a window. Street arc lamps showed only minute green flames on amber mantles. The only bright sparks in the blackness were the fiery red tail lights of the cars and the blinding blue flashes from an occasional trolley.

As stringent petrol rationing was introduced, fewer and fewer cars appeared in the streets and newspapers were filled with advertisements for cars for sale. Eventually all but twelve petrol stations in the capital were closed, a number considered sufficient for the cars still allowed to run—those with a red "V" painted on the licence plate, belonging to the privileged few, such as Nazi Party officials, doctors, high-powered industrialists. Travel by taxi was also severely regulated; one had to be on State business, crippled in some way, or traveling with four heavy pieces of luggage to ride in one legitimately.

To one observer, Berlin in the blackout seemed "like a lost city at the bottom of the sea," but to one particular group in the capital the *Verdunklung* came as a boon. It was noted that despite the Nazi ban on prostitution:

> certain girls made easy pickups . . . even the old girls, the wrinkled ones, stood on corners with their ugly features safely hidden in the darkness and shone their flashlights on their legs in invitation.

Stephen Laird, Berlin correspondent of *Time* commented on the going rates: "Some streetwalkers are available for 2/6d [38 cents], but the better-grade girls cost £5 [$15]." Elsewhere they were more expensive, however, charging as much as £35 [$105] for a full night in Garmisch.

The blackout also brought more menacing problems. In the first eighteen months of the war there had allegedly been thirty-five reported rape cases in Berlin, but many others went unreported. As Laird noted:

> Most of the cases were rapes of prostitutes out on the streets at night. A gang of soldiers just grabbed one of them in the blackout and that was that.

The suppression of such vice and immorality was a matter for official concern during that first autumn and winter of the war and areas of moral sensitivity extended beyond prostitution and crime into the world of culture, literature and entertainment. Leopold Gutterer, Goebbels' State Secretary at the Propaganda Ministry found that, while complaints about certain nightclub performances were unjustified as they did not contain "actual obscenities," there was a "very decadent dancing couple" to be found at the Frasquita nightclub on the Hardenbergstrasse. Consequently, Goebbels himself ordered that the proprietor of the Frasquita withdrew the couple. Gutterer also found the farce *Man in a Bath Tub* playing at the capital's Theater am Schiffbauerdamm in March 1940 "highly offensive and undesirable" as it consisted of nothing but *double entendres*." Yet at the same time, Joseph C. Harsch of the *Christian Science Monitor* observed: "For a country which is

(Opposite)  Margot and Hedi Hoffner dancing in cellophane dresses at the Berlin Opera House in 1940. The Swedish paper Svenska Dabladet reported on 28 April 1942 that from 1 May 1942 theater, concert and opera tickets were to be rationed, and that the public would have to register at ticket offices just as they did at the grocers. The Nazi Party tried to alleviate the situation by holding concerts and shows with dancers, singers, acrobats and comedians for soldier's wives.

(Right)  Two women athletes training with medicine balls.
"Non-political sport, so-called neutral sport, is unthinkable in the Reich of Adolf Hitler."
Guide book for German Athletics, 1936.

(Below)  German girls, helping on the land during an early wartime harvest, enjoy a midday meal.

supposed to be against sin, they seem to like their nudes rather hot and steamy,'' as he examined the display on a news-stand on the Unter den Linden. Such displays were, of course, part of a deliberate attempt to create an atmosphere of *gesunde Erotika* (healthy eroticism), designed to increase the birth rate, so important to future plans of expansion. The Nazis had loudly denounced the permissiveness of the Weimar Republic with its gay bars, nude cabarets and pornographic literature, but now as the war was getting underway, and the need to produce future soldiers for the Reich became a ''patriotic duty,'' a flood of near-pornographic nudist and naturalist literature appeared on the news-stands. At the Adlon Hotel there were to be found at least half a dozen booklets of nude photographs displayed prominently, and almost every popular magazine contained at least two or three ''nature'' photographs, posing under the guise of art or health. A typical example was ''Der schöne Mensch in der Natur,'' printed on expensive paper and containing sixteen full-page photographs of nude women; the publisher Verlag Geist und Schönheit (Spirit and Beauty) of Dresden advertised other magazines promising the purchaser ''some hundred timely pictures of open-air life, joy of living and beauty.''

Official encouragement to present the Führer with a future soldier was not slow in coming. Three months after the end of the campaign in Poland, the Christmas Eve 1939 edition of the *Berliner Morgenpost* contained the following article:

> Rudolf Hess addresses an unmarried mother: As all National Socialists know, the highest law in war, as in peace, is as follows: preservation of the Race. Every custom, law and opinion has to give way and to adapt itself to this highest law. Such an unmarried mother may have a hard path. But she knows that when we are at war; it is better to have a child under the most difficult conditions than not to have one at all. It is taken for granted today that a woman and mother who is widowed or divorced may marry again. It must also be taken for granted that a woman who has a ''war child'' may enter into marriage with a man who is not the father of that child and who sees in the woman's motherhood the foundation of marriage and companionship. The family is the basis of the country; but a race, especially during a war, cannot afford to neglect to keep and continue its national heritage . . . the highest service which a woman may perform for the community as a contribution to the continuation of the nation is to bear racially healthy children. Be happy, good woman, that you have been permitted to perform this highest duty for Germany. Be happy that the man whom you love lives in your child. Heil Hitler.

As a result of such officially-inspired appeals William Bayles, German correspondent of *Life* magazine, came across this somewhat startling advertisement:

> Two vital, lusty, race-conscious Brünnhildes with family trees certified back to 1700, desirous of serving their Fatherland in the form most ennobling to women, would like to make the acquaintance of two similarly-inclined Siegfrieds. Marriage not of essential importance. Soldiers on furlough also ''acceptable.''

Warsaw capitulated on 27 September 1939 after a period of heroic resistance, and on 6 October Hitler again addressed the Reichstag:

*The publicity brochure for Hans Bertram's* Feuertaufe *(Baptism of Fire) which showed the role of the Luftwaffe in the 1939 Polish campaign. It was released in April 1940, and was shown in cinemas in the Yorkville district of New York as late as August 1941.*

One thing is certain. In the course of world history there have never been two victors; but very often only losers. May those peoples and their leaders who are of the same opinion now make their reply. And let those who consider war to be the better solution reject my outstretched hand.

Both Chamberlain and French premier Edouard Daladier did reject that outstretched hand, and the Germans prepared to settle down to their first wartime winter, a winter not made any brighter by the complicated rationing system which came into operation on 25 September 1939 (provisional food rationing had started on 28 August). Each German family obtained seven food cards from the neighborhood ration office (*Kartenstelle*); on 6 April 1942 potatoes were rationed and an eighth card was issued. Each card was color-coded: blue cards for meat; yellow for fat and other dairy products; white for sugar, jam and marmalade; green for eggs; orange for bread; pink for flour, rice, cream of wheat, oatmeal, tea and coffee substitutes; and purple for sweets, nuts and fruits. Consumers were grouped according to the rations they were entitled to receive. Recipients of extra rations were workers in heavy industry (miners in the Ruhr were allowed $2\frac{1}{2}$ times the national average), people working long hours, expectant and nursing mothers, blood and human milk donors, sick people, and vegetarians. Each of these groups received such special extra rations as were necessitated by their special personal or working conditions. Jews, on the other hand, received severely reduced rations. The ration cards were issued for periods of four weeks (twenty-eight days), and before each distribution period the Food Ministry would notify consumers of the rations available in the new rationing period. When rationing was first introduced, an "average" German was entitled to the following each week: 1 lb (453 g) meat, 5 lb (2·2 kg) bread, 12 oz (340 g) fats, 12 oz (340 g) sugar, and 1 lb (453 g) ersatz coffee made of roasted barley

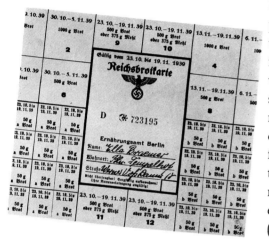

*A civilian ration card for bread covering the period 23 October to 19 November 1939. A neutral observed of the German food situation at this time: "The only item that is adequate is bread, the weekly ration of five pounds for average consumers and seven-and-a-half pounds for day workers being more than even a German labourer is accustomed to eating. . . . A common sight in the parks and wooded environs of Berlin is Germans surreptitiously discarding bags of stale bread."*

*Issuing ration tickets. An American correspondent noted in the first winter of the war: "Germans are saying that even if they do survive the war, they will undoubtedly end up in a lunatic asylum as a result of the rationing system. Trust the Germans to devise the most complicated system possible."*

*(Above)  A German worker and his family (wife and six children) eating the Sunday* Eintopf. *Germans were urged, through a heavy domestic propaganda campaign, once a month to eat a cheap "one-pot" Sunday meal and to donate the money thereby saved to the Winter Relief Fund or other social welfare "charities."*

*(Above, right)*  Eintopf *in the Reich Chancellery. In his* Berlin Diary *on 22 October 1939 American correspondent William Shirer noted: "Eintopf-one-pot-day this Sunday. Which means all you can get for lunch is a cheap stew. But you pay the price of a big meal for it, the difference going to the Winter Relief, or so they say. Actually it goes into the war chest."*

seeds and acorns. For a nation that had already given up butter for guns, the rationing system was no great hardship, and, indeed, it is estimated that some 40 per cent of the population found themselves with more than they had had in peacetime. Nevertheless, it gave birth to many sour jokes at the expense of the regime:

> What's the difference between India and Germany?
>
> In India one man starves for millions (Gandhi); in Germany millions starve for one man.

"Recipes," such as the following were a favorite:

> Take your meat ration card and fry it crisp in a mixture of your egg, flour and fat cards. Use your coal card for fuel. Serve with steamed vegetable card and boiled potato card. Pour your milk card into your coffee card, and sweeten it with your sugar card. Before enjoying your bountiful meal, treat yourself to a wash with your soap card, and dry your hands on the rest of your ration cards. Guten Appetit.

Sam Woods, Commercial Attaché at the U.S. Embassy, was witness to a less humorous aspect of the rationing system. He was in a small dairy near his flat when he heard a woman, dressed in black, begging and pleading for some pure milk. The shopkeeper was only supposed to sell pure milk to sick persons and expectant mothers on presentation of a special permit. To others he could only sell skimmed milk. The woman had started to cry. "You don't know how it is," she said in a low voice, "They brought my son home yesterday in an ambulance." All the Germans in the tiny shop were listening to her. Wearily the shopkeeper said he was sorry but he could not help. He heard such stories all day long.

> "They brought him home with both his hands gone. Blown right off, they told me." The little Hausfrau took out her handkerchief. "I can't stand it," she said. "He can't eat anything and you sell me skimmed milk."
>
> "For the love of God," the Commercial Attaché told the shopkeeper, "take my ration card and give this woman all the whole milk she wants."

''Thanks,'' said the shopkeeper, declining the card, ''I guess I can take the risk.''

After the woman had departed with a precious quart of milk, the customers in the shop—the Nazis and the non-Nazis—stared at each other coldly, each group daring the other say something.

A colleague recounted how Woods' superior at the Embassy, Chargé d'Affaires Alexander Kirk, had first encountered the next phase of rationing, clothes rationing:

> Braun's is an ultra-smart store for men's clothes on Unter den Linden, the kind of place where the cheapest handkerchief costs one dollar (25p). Kirk had slept two weeks straight at the Embassy; he decided to buy himself a fresh pair of pyjamas. Walking out for a breath of air, he wandered into Braun's, and asked a yawning clerk to show him several pairs of pyjamas. The clerk refused politely. ''We are not allowed to sell anything until the ration cards come out,'' he said. Our Chargé d'Affaires identified himself, and explained that he really needed pyjamas. The clerk was impressed, but he had his orders. Resigning himself to the situation, Alexander Kirk started to leave. Near the door, he looked at a bunch of neckties on display. He fingered one tentatively. ''I am sorry,'' the clerk recited. ''We can't sell any neckties either.'' He departed. The Chargé d'Affaires of the United States, many times over a millionaire couldn't even buy a necktie.

Actual clothes rationing was introduced on 16 November 1939. Each German was issued with a clothing card (*Kleiderkarte*). The one for the first year of the war consisted of coupons totaling 100 points, with so many to be clipped off for each rationed item. There were 150 points on the card for the second year, and 120 points for the third year of the war, but the number required for each article of clothing had so changed that one bought about the same on each card. The number on the 150-point basis was sufficient unless major items, such as a suit, were required—a suit required 80 points on a man's card and had to be made out of a piece of cloth exactly 3·1 meters by 144 centimeters (3·3 by 1·5 yards). When those 80 points had been used, a man would have enough left for no more than two shirts, a suit of summer underwear, and two pairs of socks. To acquire a new overcoat, one had to deliver the old one to the dealer to prove that it could no longer be used. To get an overcoat without sacrificing the old one would cost 120 out of 150 points in the winter of 1940. The following schedule of points required for clothing on the 1940 150 points card shows how carefully the German male had to plan his clothing needs for the year:

| | |
|---|---|
| Suit | 80 |
| Trousers | 28 |
| Vest (heavy) | 42 |
| Vest (light) | 28 |
| Sweater | 21 |
| Pullover (short sleeve) | 16 |
| Raincoat | 25 |
| Top coat | 65 |

*A woman's* Reichskleiderkarte— *clothing card.*

ARWA
auf Taille  der Strumpf mit den
formgebenden Taillenlinien!

Bezugsquellennachweis durch:
ARWA VERKAUFSBÜRO · CHEMNITZ · Dresdner Straße 36

| | |
|---|---|
| Overcoat | 120 |
| Gloves | 5 |
| Shirt | 20, 22, 24, according to size |
| Polo shirt | 12–15 |
| Nightshirt | 19–30 |
| Undershirt | 11–14 |
| Pyjamas | 29–45 |
| Underpants | 14–18 |
| Socks | 4–8 |
| Bathing trunks | 12–15 |
| Bathing gown | 30 |
| Handkerchief | 1 |
| Collar | 1 |
| Tie | 1 |

When buying a suit most Germans usually bought a ready-made one. They were not always a good fit and, as an observer noticed, were always made ''with seats far too ample.'' Because of the way they were manufactured and the quality of the material, they would not press well and tended to wear out quickly. None was pure wool, and most were of substitute or synthetic materials usually processed from wood and other such substances. Germans who could afford it bought tailored suits from stores such as Braun's, or Dietl's, tailors to the former Royal House of Hohenzollern. Such suits cost at least 300 marks (75 dollars at the 1939 rate of exchange) in 1940, whereas a pre-war tailored suit cost 120 marks (less than 30 dollars). Those with enough money or influence were able to obtain real wool from the limited stocks.

Some Germans valued their clothing cards so lightly that one chauffeur at the Berlin radio station offered an American correspondent, Harry W. Flannery, his card if Flannery would sell him two of his suits.

The clothing system for women was more complicated, partly because of the greater variety of materials. Most women, for instance, wore rayon, lisle, or cotton stockings in winter, and none in summer, when often the ''seam'' was painted on bare legs. After the fall of France a glut of silk stockings appeared. A woman was permitted four pairs of stockings a year, at the beginning of the war, at four points per pair. If she wanted more, she then had to sacrifice eight points for each additional pair.The complexities of the points system on a woman's card were highlighted by the fact that a wool dress required 56 points, one of artificial silk 25, and one of any other material 36. Simplified, the required points in 1940 were as shown below:

| | |
|---|---|
| Gown | 23–42 |
| Suit | 25–56 |
| Skirt | 10–18 |
| Sweater | 9–19 |
| Vest | 18–23 |
| Raincoat | 25 |
| Summer coat | 45–50 |

| Winter coat | 100 |
| --- | --- |
| Apron | 10–12 |
| Scarf | 4–8 |
| Shirt | 7–12 |
| Nightgown | 16–22 |
| Petticoat | 7–14 |
| Brassiere | 10–14 |
| Stockings | 4 |
| Bathing costume | 12–15 |
| Underclothes | 8–14 |
| Knickers | 10 |
| Girdle | 8 |
| Bathing gown | 30 |
| Handkerchief | 1 |

Children under seventeen could obtain an additional clothing card because they outgrew their clothes. These cards provided 50 extra points for boys and 40 extra for girls.

Shoes could only be purchased by obtaining a permit from the rationing office. Before one could receive such a permit (*Bezugschein*), a declaration had to be made that the applicant had only two pairs of shoes, and of the two, one pair had to be shown to be beyond the possibility of repair. Officials sometimes made random checks to make certain that claimants, especially women, were telling the truth. If more were found, they were confiscated, and the owner liable to a fine. Real leather for repairs began to disappear and was soon only available for the privileged few and some foreigners. An American paid 12 marks 80 pfennings ($3.20) for a small

*In wartime Germany the shortage of raw materials severely handicapped the manufacture of shoes. With the exception of wood for soles, no really durable substitute for leather was found. Consequently considerable effort went into drives and schemes to collect and re-use old leather. Here children try on shoes at an exchange center set up by the Women's Organization.*

repair in leather and had to wait six weeks before the work was done; (a skilled worker on average received 60 marks a week, an unskilled one 30 marks). Most Germans had to put up with an inferior substitute which often barely lasted one month. Many women decided on wooden soles which did not wear out, and which could be obtained without a *Bezugschein* until the summer of 1941, when they too were only sold with a permit.

Dry cleaning of clothes again proved difficult, with it often taking up to a month before the garments were returned. For washing clothes the *Hausfrau* was able to get only 250 grammes, or about half a pound of soap powder a month. A woman with a family therefore usually had to let the washing accumulate for a month, which was difficult because it was almost impossible to get a sufficient stock of clothes. Toilet soap was also rationed: each person was allowed five fifty-gramme cakes for four months (about two ounces a month). The soap was a dull greyish-green color, harsh and gritty, and made a thick scum in the water. Perversely, Hitler praised the wartime soap to intimates at his table on 18 August 1942: "With this wartime soap, I can wash my hands as often as I like without fear of a cracked skin ... but with the old peacetime soap I became very sore." Others were less complimentary, and by the autumn of 1941 American radio reporter Howard K. Smith observed:

> To see the people you take a subway. You also smell them. There is not enough time nor enough coaches for coaches to be properly cleaned and ventilated every day, so the odor of stale sweat from bodies that work hard, and have only a cube of soap as big as a penny box of matches to wash with for a month, lingers in their interiors and is reinforced quantitatively until it changes for the worse, qualitatively as time and war proceed. In summer, it is asphyxiating ... dozens of people, whose stomachs and bodies are not strong anyhow, faint in them every day. Sometimes you just have to get out at some station halfway to your destination to take a breath of fresh air between trains.

To eke out the soap ration, official advice was to wet the hands thoroughly before using the soap as one used less than when soap and water were combined at the same time. Almost every German household had a grilled block on which to keep soap in order that it would not be wasted by standing in water in an ordinary soap tray. For men one cake of shaving soap or a tube of shaving cream had to last four months. Chemical preparations of shaving cream and facial soap were sold everywhere, but all lacked the necessary oils. To get a shave at a barbers usually involved queuing for up to an hour, which gave rise to the quip that the price of shaves would soon increase because since the beginning of the war men's faces had become longer. The *Völkischer Beobachter* advised its readers that for a bath soap was not necessary if one took pine needles, stewed them and poured off the liquid to use in the tub. Not only did it cut the dirt, the paper claimed, but it was good for easing rheumatism. Other "natural" aid hints included powdered chestnut meal for face and hands, and ivy leaves, it was claimed, when stewed and strained, were more than adequate for laundering clothes. Babies received a special ration of better soap. Toilet paper fared no better than soap, becoming an early casualty of the war. In October 1939 a correspondent's maid tried half a dozen shops on and off for a week without success,

*A bottle collection depot for the Wehrmacht, 1939. American correspondent Lothrop Stoddard noted in October 1939: "Every family is in duty bound not to waste anything. So each German kitchen has a covered pail into which goes all garbage that can be served to pigs ... what we in America call 'trash' must be carefully segregated into the following categories (1) newspapers, magazines, or other clean paper (2) rags (3) bottles (4) old metal (5) broken furniture or just about anything else that is thrown away. City collectors come around for this segregated trash at regular intervals."*

in the end commenting that they would have to save up the *Völkischer Beobachter*. Equally ribald remarks were made concerning the millions of leaflets dropped by the RAF.

The influx of goods from the conquered lands in 1940–41 helped to alleviate the situation somewhat, but by late 1941 they had begun to run out; trains were now arriving at Berlin stations with very different cargoes. At the Potsdamer Bahnhof in late 1941 the three easternmost lines were filled with long trains, each coach marked with the Red Cross: hospital trains carrying wounded Germans from the Eastern Front to hospitals in Berlin. The change in the fortunes of war naturally provoked comparisons. As a drunken old Berliner pointed out to Howard K. Smith: "From France we got silk stockings. From Russia we got this. Damned Russians must not have any silk stockings, eh?"

Tobacco requisites were also war casualties, and supplies remained inadequate and uncertain throughout the war; long queues were to be found at tobacconists lucky enough to obtain supplies. Two or three small inferior cigars were the usual ration. Christmas shopping in December 1939 John McCutcheon Raleigh went to the cigar section of Awag's department store (formerly the Jewish-owned Wertheim's):

> Four or five pillars of display boxes stood on the counter. All of them contained paper replicas of popular brands of cigars and cigarettes. The shelves behind them were empty. The assistant continually repeated that this or that brand of smokes were sold out. He earned his money with a vengeance, for nearly everyone had some unpleasant remark to make about the shortage.

One could also obtain pipe tobacco "like a poor grade of mattress filling," according to one smoker; the best brand was Dunhill which on reading the small

*(Previous pages) German police troops supervise Polish women forced to unload supplies at the station of Wlochy.*

print was found to have been ''Made in Germany.'' A similar deception was practised with cigarettes, which sold from 40 pfennigs (10 cents) to 1 mark 60 pfennigs (40 cents) a packet, with no more than five cigarettes being allowed to each customer. In some places cigarettes were not available for women smokers. Juno was a popular brand in Berlin, and other favorites included Kemal, Lord Chesterfield, Aristons, Murattis, and North State, which was claimed to be a product of Philip Morris, one of the leading U.S. cigarette manufacturers of the time. A year before America entered the war a bogus brand called ''Cocktail American Bridge Club'' said to have been made by the ''United Cigarette Factories Inc, Empire State Building, New York, U.S.A.'' appeared briefly on the market.

The quality of cigarettes suffered as the war progressed. The brand Johnnies changed flavor no less than three times in one year, according to one smoker, who recalled how the most marked change had occurred after General Rommel's occupation of Cyrenaica when rumor had it that the main ingredient was now camel dung—the first booty from the latest occupied territory.

To discourage smoking the authorities started publishing anti-smoking propaganda—''The Führer does not smoke'' (but Goebbels did—as many as sixty a day)—and Hitler Youths were given lectures on the harm done by smoking to their bodies, which had to be preserved ''for Führer and Fatherland.'' Women were also heavily discouraged—''The German woman does not smoke''—and restaurants and cafés were forbidden to sell cigarettes to women customers. Eventually, in February 1942, a uniform system of tobacco rationing was introduced throughout the Reich by means of smokers' control cards. By August 1943 the following five alternatives were being offered to smokers:

| | |
|---|---|
| Cigarettes | 6 for 2 days |
| Cigars (6 pfennigs) | 12 for 10 days |
| Cigars (7–12 pfennigs) | 9 for 10 days |
| Cigars (12 pfennigs) | 6 for 10 days |
| Tobacco | $1\frac{3}{4}$ oz for 14 days |

*A cartoon dating from 1940, and characteristically robust in its humor shows the British premier making paper ships and planes out of old copies of* The Times—*now used as a toilet paper substitute, just as indeed the* Völkischer Beobachter *was in Germany—to replace those lost by enemy action.*

Standardized cigarettes were introduced in July 1943, and extra rations were always issued after air raids.

The war also brought an ''alcoholic drought,'' and in the early months it was almost impossible to find cognac or other spirits, although wine and champagne remained fairly plentiful. The first complaints about watered-down beer were heard quite early on in the war, and William D. Bayles recalled ''I received a glass . . . that would have made any Bavarian *Braumeister* blush with shame.'' He continued:

> It was announced some time ago that the amount of grain allowed for beer had been restricted, and with the demand increasing, there is no solution but the water-tap. Certain famous breweries are to receive permission to keep their quality at par and to increase the price as the supply of grain is reduced . . .

Supplies of wines, spirits and liqueurs rose dramatically with the conquest of the Low Countries and France in the spring and summer of 1940, and as late as March 1943 some Berlin restaurants could boast very impressive wine lists. Spirits stocks

*The sheet music to the battle song "Bomben auf Engelland" with music by Norbert Schultze whose most famous composition was "Lili Marleen." "Bomben auf Engelland" was featured in the propaganda film* Feuertaufe *(Baptism of Fire), directed by Hans Bertram, which lauded the role of the Luftwaffe in the Polish campaign.*

were soon exhausted, however, and the Russian campaign brought further dramatic changes to the drinks trade. By official order production of beer was lowered 20 per cent, and taverns and bars started closing one day a week. By the end of 1941 "there were only four places in all Berlin where one could get beer consistently, and their supplies were maintained for sheer propaganda effect, the biggest hotels and the (foreign) press clubs." But even in those places drinking hours were set, outside of which beer could not be obtained.

Even the Adlon Hotel began watering its beer. At the rival Kaiserhof the bar had an empty counter, but with a display of bottles of colored water against its mirrored background. Howard K. Smith observed:

> It caused visible pain to the old bartender to answer an order for a cocktail saying he was dreadfully sorry, but today, precisely today, he had run out of ingredients . . . actually all he had was some raw liquor the management had been able to squeeze out of a farmhouse outside Berlin, *Himbeergeist*, (raspberry syrup—usually added to a *Berliner Weisse* beer), or a fake vodka that took the roof off your mouth, or wood alcohol with perfume in it . . . served under the name of "*Sclibovitz*."

*(Opposite, above) Munich, 8 November 1939: Hitler finishes his speech in the Bürgerbräukeller. Ten minutes later a bomb exploded in a column just behind the podium. Hitler had left the hall earlier than anticipated and thus escaped almost certain death. The bomb, planted by carpenter and Communist sympathizer Georg Elser, killed 7 and wounded 63, including Eva Braun's father.*

*(Opposite, below) The Bürgerbräukeller after the explosion. Hitler exclaimed on learning the news: "Now I am completely content! The fact that I left the Bürgerbräukeller earlier than usual is a corroboration of Providence's intention to let me reach my goal." It was later maintained that the assassination attempt had been wholly engineered by Hitler to increase his own popularity and kindle the patriotic fervor of the people. It remains a controversial issue to this day.*

In most bars a standard cocktail was instituted under various names: "Razzle-dazzle," "Hollywood" (before Pearl Harbor) or "Extase." The mixture usually remained the same: "a shot of some kind of raw, stomach-searing alcohol with a generous dilution of thick grenadine syrup."

Other places used the Kaiserhof trick of colored water and were consequently often besieged by eager would-be customers. A delicatessen on the Kurfürstendamm had to place a notice in its window: "These bottles are filled with colored water and nothing else. They are purely for the purposes of decoration. We have no liquor, so please do not bother our sales staff; we are short-handed due to the war."

In shop windows, displays not only of alcohol but all other goods were maintained, the idea being, by some strange quirk, to keep up morale. These displays were labeled "Nur Attrapen" ("for decoration only") and usually had a small card down in the corner which stated that the contents might not be sold until the decorations were changed. Dairies displayed rows of milk bottles, seven-eighths full of white salt to look like milk. One shopkeeper, to relieve the monotony of these displays, incurred official disapproval by putting not empty boxes in the windows, but a big profile photograph of Hitler with a gilt swastika above it, and below it, in gold letters: "We thank our Führer!" And when the German-staffed American Express Company was forced to close as a reprisal, the employees

> took a last bitter crack at the Nazis . . . by sticking up a poster saying "Visit Medieval Germany."

During the long, bleak, first winter of the war attempts were made to keep up morale and engender a hatred of the enemy, and according to an official report such propaganda bore fruit:

> People are aware that England is Germany's main enemy and the general mood is so solidly against England that even children in the streets are singing satirical songs about England and especially about Chamberlain.

One such example, "Our Father Chamberlain," a parody of the Lord's prayer, was even broadcast on the radio. And a similar religious parody turned the carol "Silent Night" into a Nazi anthem.

On 8 November the Führer was the target of an assassination attempt in the "Bürgerbräu" cellar in Munich on the occasion of the annual reunion of *Alte Kämpfer* (Old fighters) in commemoration of the abortive Beer Hall Putsch of 1923. The assassination attempt was not indicative of any great resentment of Hitler, however. An SD (*Sicherheitsdienst*, Security Service of the SS) report commented:

> The attempted assassination in Munich has strengthened the people's feeling of solidarity. Public interest in the results of the special commission's inquiry into the event is very great. The question of how it could have happened remains the number one topic of conversation in all social circles. Love for the Führer has grown even stronger and the attitude toward the war has become more positive in many circles as a result . . .

Pope Pius XII sent Hitler a congratulatory letter, but others took a less benevolent view: "Boy, if it had worked, we'd all be dead drunk under the table by now," said one of Ruth Andreas-Friedrich's anti-Nazi circle, and a milkman in Berlin felt that: "Germany was cursed with the worst luck of any nation on earth."

*Germany's Gaue, September 1942.*

The harsh winter, the worst for many years, continued. Everywhere people jested that the icy cold weather had been thrown in gratis by the Russians along with the Non-Aggression Pact! Shirer recorded in his diary on 9 January 1940:

> This has been one of the coldest days I've experienced in fourteen years in Europe. Tens of thousands of homes and many offices are without coal. Real suffering among many. With the rivers and canals, which transport most of the coal, frozen over, the Germans can't bring in adequate supplies.

Nevertheless, both Christmas and New Year had been celebrated with something like pre-war gaiety. Goebbels sourly commented: ''Berlin society is still celebrating merrily, as if the war had nothing to do with them. The dregs! To the rubbish heap with them!'' But indeed to many it seemed difficult to believe that a war was on.

60

The streets and parks are covered deep with snow and in the Tiergarten this afternoon thousands were skating on the ponds and lagoons. Hundreds of children were tobogganing. Do children think about war? I don't know. This afternoon in the Tiergarten they seemed to be thinking only of their sledges and skates and the snow and ice,

mused Shirer on 28 January. A fortnight earlier an American diplomat had told a colleague how he was standing in the snow reading film placards on one of the many street advertising columns. A propaganda poster was also plastered on the column:

An old Berlin worker with black ear muffs and a red nose walked up . . . and began to spell out the words on the poster to a companion: "Nobody shall Hunger or Freeze" the poster stated. "Hell," the older Berliner grumbled, "even *that* is *verboten* now!"

Eventually spring showed signs of arriving, as Shirer recorded on 18 March:

Millions of Germans are beginning to thaw out after the worst winter they can remember. For some reason there was no hot water in most apartments today, though it was Sunday. Several friends lined up in my room for a bath.

Some three weeks later, Germany invaded Norway and Denmark on 9 April. The controlled Press responded enthusiastically. *Der Angriff* that day announced: "The young German Army has hoisted new glory to its banners . . . It is one of the most brilliant feats of all time." The *Börsen Zeitung* justified the invasion: "England steps coldbloodedly over the dead bodies of small peoples. Germany protects the weak states from the English highwaymen." The following day the *Völkischer Beobachter* headlined: "Germany saves Scandinavia!"

*German anti-gas preparations in the early part of the war. Germany had initiated gas warfare during the First World War. A "people's mask" was distributed to the population but on a much smaller scale than in Great Britain where 38 million masks had been issued during the Munich Crisis.*

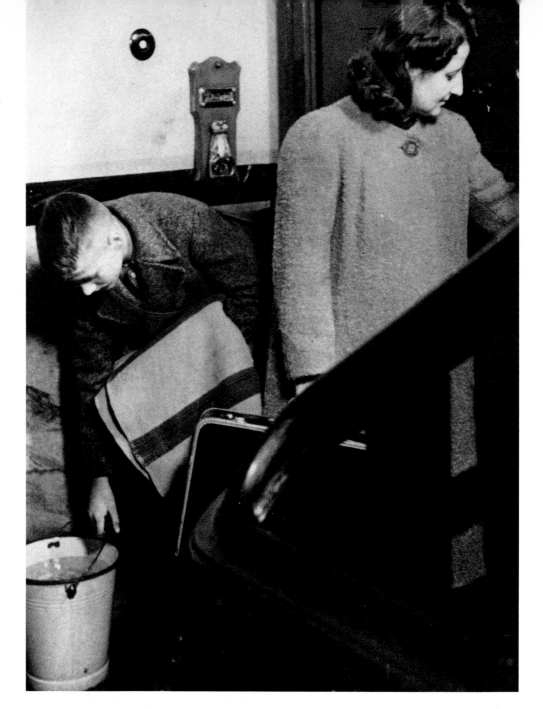

A month later at 5.30 am on 10 May 1940 German troops marched into neutral
Holland, Belgium and Luxembourg thereby beginning, in the Führer's words, "the
battle that will decide the future of the German nation for the next thousand years."
Six weeks later the Wehrmacht had reached Paris and the French were suing for an
armistice. Joseph C. Harsch described the victory atmosphere:

> Victories had an astounding lack of power to rouse enthusiasm. The day
> Paris fell (14 June) they put up some big loudspeakers in the Wilhelmplatz
> . . . the loudspeakers blared national and party songs. But I counted just
> about 100 people in that whole big square. The music stopped. The excited,
> triumphant voice of the radio announcer came over the air. Paris had fallen.
> German troops were marching into the Place de la Concorde. Then
> *Deutschland über Alles.* The little groups of people put up their right arms

German air raid precautions or
Luftschutz *supervised by the*
Reichsluftschutzbund *were well
advanced when the first Allied bombs
hit German cities in the summer of
1940. The RLB had a few thousand
professional members and thirteen
million volunteers by 1939. Realistic air
raid drills had taken place in most cities
and a law passed as early as 1935
declared that "all Germans will be
obliged to render such services as are
necessary for the execution of air
defense." These photographs, show
German civilians undergoing basic civil
defense precautions and shelter drill.*

*Makeshift beds in the shelter where
people can try to get some sleep.*

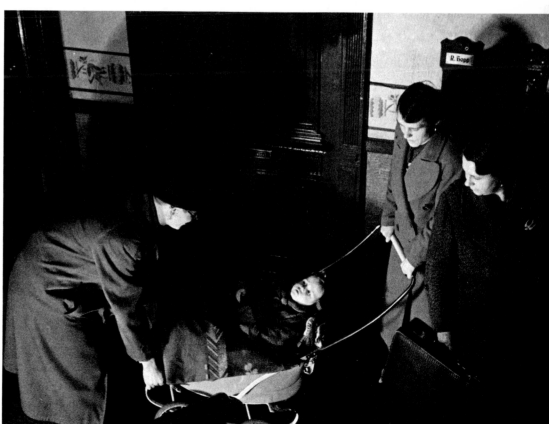

*Neighbors help a mother and child down
into the cellar before an air raid.*

in perfunctory Nazi salutes. The loudspeakers went silent and everyone walked away. Not a sound of cheering. Not an exclamation of pleasure.

They just walked off as though nothing of importance had happened. Shirer was sunbathing at the Bad Hallensee, a swimming pool just on the edge of Berlin, when some newsboys burst on the scene with extras shouting about the fall of Paris. They sold exactly three copies. It was just the same with the French armistice—newspapers published extra editions, but found few takers. Nevertheless there was deep satisfaction at the triumph of German arms throughout the Reich. The *Landrat* (District Magistrate) of Mainz reported that "the domestic position of the State has never been stronger." He knew, of course, of a few grumblers who had not considered it necessary to fly the flag, and others who were more worried "about how to obtain ration cards than about the results of military battles." But even for these Germans, considered too materialistic by good Nazis, the military triumphs brought an increase in rations: after 1 July an additional quarter of a pound of butter per person was issued. Furthermore, an improvement in the quality of beer was introduced by raising the basic wort from 6 per cent to 9–10 per cent to create "a better disposition among these numerous German beer drinkers who frequently criticized the quality of their favorite beverage."

Hitler returned to the capital in triumph on 6 July and was received with hysterical excitement. Joseph C. Harsch did not stay for the entire ceremony, but went instead with a U.S. Embassy official to a small lake for a swim. The regular public beaches were closed that day, but on this private one, there were "more than its usual quota of sunbathers and swimmers, who sat around or splashed in the water exactly as though nothing out of the ordinary was happening."

Some of these same sunbathers had incurred the wrath of Goebbels, who the following day ordered Gutterer to instruct the police to make one or two raids on the Wannsee and the adjacent lakes to confiscate all English gramophone records along with the gramophones themselves. As for their owners, a check should be made to see whether they were listed as employees in "reserved occupations," and whether any could be transferred to labor squads. The Minister described it as "a scandal that jazz music with English words should be publicy disseminated in the English language during the war". He considered one or two such operations sufficient to make their mark upon the circles concerned.

Of Germany's enemies only Britain now remained unconquered, and soon the Luftwaffe was flung into the Battle of Britain in an attempt to wipe out the RAF before invasion. The battle was not one-sided. On 25 August the Royal Air Force bombed the capital for the first time (previously a French naval aircraft the *Jules Verne* had bombed the city's outskirts on 7 June). According to Shirer the Berliners were stunned, not expecting it to happen. Further raids followed and on 28 August ten persons were killed and twenty-nine wounded, the first casualties in the capital. The RAF also dropped leaflets telling the populace that "the war which Hitler started will go on, and it will last as long as Hitler does." The SD reported that there was unrest among the population in western Germany who had been exposed to British raids for some time and Bamberg's Public Prosecutor General penned the following inauspicious report:

W. C. der neue Gott der Griechen

Der alte Zeus ward einst zum Stier
Weil er verstrickt in Eros Schlingen,
Und die Verwandlung tat gelingen,
Damit Europa er entführ.
Doch einem Rindvieh macht's Beschwerden,
Nun umgekehrt zum Gott zu werden.

*Italy invaded Greece on 28 October 1940 expecting a* Blitzkrieg *campaign but Greek resistance was such that Germany had to bail out her ally in April 1941. Prior to this the British had sent RAF Squadrons to aid the Greeks. Here* Der Stürmer *satirizes Churchill as the "New Greek God," in its 21 November 1940 issue.*

> That segment of the population without real political insight or positive
> political behavior has not proved to be so insignificant. This group, which
> previously shared a common optimism, given the brilliant military
> victories . . . is now viewing a second winter of war with mistrust and
> pusillanimity after these little air raid alarms and bombings. . . .

The *Berliner Börsen Zeitung* of 31 August christened the RAF bomber crews ''air
pirates,'' and concentration camp inmates were used to perform bomb disposal
duties after the raids.

Whilst the newspapers foamed with indignation at ''the British island of
murderers,'' who would ''have to take the consequences of its malicious bombings''
(*Berliner Zeitung am Mittag* 19 September 1940), the authorities themselves were
killing thousands of Germans in a Hitler-approved euthanasia scheme which,
between January 1940 and August 1941, accounted for the deaths of 70,273 of the
Reich's mentally ill. The scheme was stopped in August 1941 after protests from
leading churchmen, particularly Bishop Clemens August von Galen of Munster,
who in St Lamberti's Church on 3 August 1941 denounced the scheme from the
pulpit as a violation of the fifth commandment.

The raids continued throughout the autumn and winter of 1940 and the *Blitz* on
England was presented as a reprisal, but as Shirer noted on 8 October:

> The German press harps so much on the Luftwaffe attacks on Britain being
> reprisals . . . that the public is already nauseated by the term—and
> Germans take a lot of nauseating. The story around town is that the average
> Berliner, when he buys his ten-pfennig evening newspaper, now says to
> the newsboy: ''Give me ten pfennigs' worth of reprisals.''

Although the capital was often raided, the Rhineland was visited by the RAF nearly
every night and as a result Berlin hotels were full of Rhineland industrialists intent
on sleep. Indeed, the Press advised people to go to bed early to get some sleep before
the RAF arrived, a suggestion that was generally met with great derision. Wits
interpreted greetings in the shelter in the following manner: ''Good morning'' meant
the person had dutifully gone to bed as advised; ''Good evening'' meant that the
person had not been to bed; ''Heil Hitler'' meant the person was still asleep!

Nonetheless, despite continued British resistance and the RAF raids, Shirer noted:

> After a year and a half of actual total war German morale is still good. . . .
> There is no popular enthusiasm for the war. There never was. And after
> eight years of deprivation caused by Nazi preparation for war, the people
> are weary and fatigued. They crave peace. They are disappointed,
> depressed, disillusioned that peace did not come this fall, as promised. Yet
> as the war goes into its second long dark winter, public morale is fairly
> high.

In Cologne the appeals court president too noted ''the increasing emotional strain
and irascibility among wide circles of the population'' but also that ''the Führer's
prestige . . . was in no way affected, likewise hardly anyone doubted a victorious
end to the war.'' And in his New Year's message Hitler announced that ''the year
1941 will consummate the greatest victory in our history.''

*(Above, left) "Another victim of the Bromberg bloodbath" read the original caption to this 1939 photograph showing Polish prisoners burying a Volksdeutscher. Nazi propaganda claimed that in the first week of the war the Poles murdered some 58,000 Germans in the Polish Corridor, the worst massacre supposedly taking place in Bromberg on 3 September 1939.*

*German naval artillerymen washing their clothes.*

*(Above) Warsaw capitulated on 27 September 1939, and the last Polish garrisons at Modlin and Hela surrendered on 5 October. 650,000 Polish prisoners such as these men were taken, many destined to become little more than agricultural serfs on German farms for the next five years.*

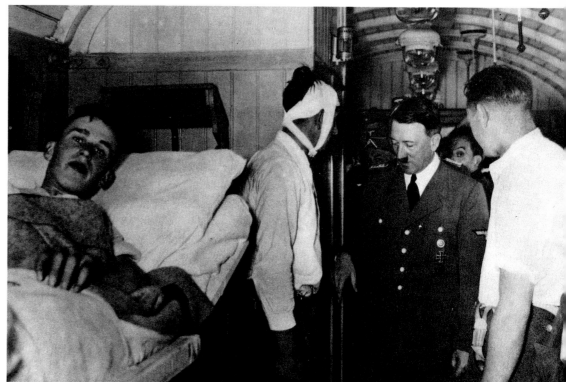

(Above) Jubilant Danzigers greet
Wehrmacht troops as they enter the city
reunited with the Reich on 1 September
1939.

(Right) September 1939. Hitler visits
German wounded in a hospital train on
the Eastern Front.

*Creche facilities were established by the Women's Organization for the children of working mothers. In May 1942 a "Law for the Protection of Motherhood" was passed which stated that expectant mothers should no longer work overtime, do night shifts, or work on Sundays or holidays.*

*(Below)  A housing estate for Reich Post Office employees in Berlin-Rudnow built just before the war. Besides encouraging employers to house their workers, the Nazis developed another answer to the post-First-World-War housing shortage, the* Volkswohnung *(the people's flat). Regulations stipulated that a childless couple needed 26 square meters and a family of four, 34 square meters. In the Weimar period, the average had been 40 square meters; the British standard in 1936 was 50 square meters.*

(Above)  The procession celebrating "2000 years of German culture" in Munich, July 1939. Anti-Nazi Ulrich von Hassell recorded "Eyewitnesses give a comical description of the condition of Hitler's rostrum during the festival. Because of the downpour the canvas roof—the blue 'heaven'—had to be propped up with poles, whereupon veritable streams of water poured down upon the rostrum. Hitler was in a very bad temper, having sent his raincoat over to his 'friend' Fraulein [Eva] Braun."

(Right)  Berliners examine the railway carriage in which the 1918 and 1940 armistices were signed at Compiègne. It was moved to Berlin in July 1940 and exhibited in the Lustgarten to raise money for the Winter Relief Fund. Ironically, the carriage was destroyed by Allied Bombing in April 1944.

(Opposite) Hitler addresses the crowd at a pre-war Nuremberg rally.

*A Polish-Jewish laborer at work.*

*Citizens in an occupied Polish city board a tram "for Jews only."*

*Hitler Youth, at a rally, carrying the special Hitler Youth Banner.*

*A mass demonstration on the Wilhelmplatz in Berlin, the Kaiserhof Hotel in the background. The Kaiserhof was where Hitler had always stayed in Berlin before becoming Chancellor, and it was from the hotel that he went to Hindenburg to receive office on 30 January 1933. It was hit by incendiary bombs in 1943 and burned to the ground.*

(Right) Old iron and metalware was collected throughout the Reich for recycling into weapons. Here German armament workers are shown at work in one of the Reich's numerous factories.

(Below) "While fanatical war fever hots up in Poland—under British protection—life goes on as normal in Germany" was the tenor of the original caption to this photograph showing tram repairs in Berlin. The tram's destination is Spandau, the site of the prison where Nazi war criminals Hess, Speer, von Schirach, Funk, Dönitz, von Neurath, and Raeder were imprisoned in 1946, and where Hess allegedly committed suicide in August 1987.

A Hitler Youth parade in Danzig, 1939.
"The Reich Youth Leader (Baldur von
Schirach) in a radio speech tonight said
that the principle of voluntary
membership in the Hitler Youth will
never be abandoned. He who comes to
the Hitler Youth must do so of his own
free will, without any compulsion."
Berliner Börsen Zeitung, 30 August 1934.

"All boys from the age of ten to eighteen
must belong to the Hitler Youth. Parents
who prevent their sons from entering the
Hitler Youth will be punished."
Von Schirach, 5 April 1939.

*(Right) Members of the Nazi Party's women's organization, the* Nationalsozialistische Frauenschaft *waiting to board the pleasure cruiser* Tannenberg *for a short holiday in recognition of their good work.*

*(Below) Germans from the Baltic States, Latvia, Lithuania and Estonia "return to the Reich" in the winter of 1939–40.*

(Right) A Baltic German girl packing prior to evacuation "home to the Reich" during the winter of 1939–40. Some 135,000 Germans from Russian-occupied eastern Poland and 100,000 Germans from the Baltic States, (Latvia, Lithuania and Estonia) were resettled in the parts of Poland that Hitler had annexed outright to the "Greater German Reich."

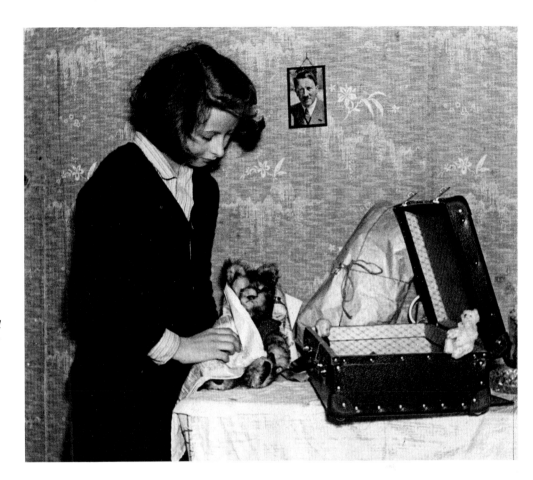

(Below, right) The front cover of a German passport: all those held by Jews were stamped inside with a purple "J." The Nazis permitted foreign travel to all but a few thousand Germans "who were in the black book of the secret police." However, such travel was severely curtailed by the stringent currency restrictions on account of the Reich's lack of foreign exchange.

(Below) A Nazi Party membership book.

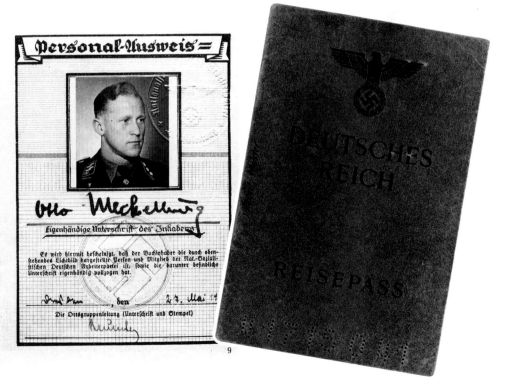

*(Right)* The anti-Semitic newspaper Der Stürmer's pre-war circulation was 500,000, and paper was still allocated to it until almost the end of the war. Julius Streicher, its editor and erstwhile Gauleiter of Franconia, was hanged at Nuremberg on 16 October 1946. Here is a photograph of the paper's Danzig office showing anti-Semitic propaganda in the window. The poster reads ''The Jews are our misfortune.''

*(Below)* A synagogue in Danzig festooned with Nazi anti-Semitic slogans: ''The synagogue will be demolished'' and ''Come dear May and make us free from the Jews.''

*(Opposite)* The Berghof, Hitler's home on the Obersalzberg above Berchtesgaden. Eva Braun nicknamed it the ''Grand Hotel,'' and for thousands of Germans before the war it became a place of pilgrimage. It was bombed by the RAF in 1945, burnt out by the SS, and the ruins finally blown up by the Americans in 1950 to prevent it from becoming a Nazi shrine.

*(Inset)* The Führer as Godfather. Hitler with Emmy Goering and her daughter Edda, born on 2 June 1938 and named after Mussolini's daughter Edda, Countess Ciano. Before her marriage to Goering on 10 April 1935, Emmy had been an actress in the repertory company of the Weimar National Theater.

(Opposite) The front cover of the Kölnische Illustrierte Zeitung 5 December 1940 showing Hitler with his designated successor Goering. Described by Hitler as being "ice cool" in a crisis, by 1945 Goering was in total disgrace, and after the Dresden disaster that February Goebbels told his staff "If I had the authority I would have this cowardly and good-for-nothing Reichsmarschall tried. He should be put before a People's Court."

(Right) A blonde archetypal Aryan member of the BDM (League of German maidens) in athletic kit. "My Führer wants me to marry. Therefore I want a young evangelical girl, of pure Aryan breed, blonde, slim but well developed, wealthy." Advertisement in the Königsberger Zeitung, 26 October 1934.

An Aryan mother and child "ideal" as shown in the 1941 yearbook of the Nazi women's organization. Mother's Day during the Third Reich was celebrated in May, and from 1939 mothers with large families were presented with the Mutterkreuz—the "Cross of Motherhood"—in recognition of their honored role.

Preis **20** Pfg.

5. Dezember 1940
Nummer 49 / 15. Jahrg.
Druck und Verlag von M.
DuMont Schauberg, Köln
Auslandspreise siehe Fuß der Rückseite

# Kölnische Illustrierte Zeitung

Heldenkampf unserer Zerstörer
FORTSETZUNG DES GROSSEN NARVIK-BERICHTS

## Freude über den Sieg!

Ein bisher nicht veröffentlichtes Bild des Führers und des Reichsmarschalls, aufgenommen nach der französischen Kapitulation

La victoire décisive cause la joie la plus intense! / Photo jusqu'alors inédite représentant le Führer et le Maréchal du Reich immédiatement après la capitulation de la France

*(Above)  An obituary notice in a
German newspaper recording the death
in action of three brothers for "Führer
and Fatherland." Many people hostile to
the regime made a point of omitting
"For Führer" when inserting death
notices in the press.*

*(Right)  A member of the fire brigade
extinguishing fires from incendiary
bombs in Berlin 1940.*

*(Opposite)  Bomb damage inside a
German home, 1940.*

# 1941–1942

*Children in an air raid shelter awaiting the all-clear.*

# "No butter with our eats"

**T**he year 1941 opened with the *Deutschlandsender*'s midnight broadcast of the bells of Cologne Cathedral, promptly followed by a rousing rendition of the Nazi Party's anthem, the *Horst Wessel Lied*. The old year had seen spectacular military victories with all Germany's enemies supressed with the exception of the British who, heartened by President Roosevelt's re-election in November and his promise that America was to be the "arsenal of Democracy," still held out defiantly in the face of the nightly blitz on their cities. The early months of 1941 brought fresh victories to the Wehrmacht. In February General Erwin Rommel, soon to become the most popular of military leaders, landed in North Africa with his *Afrika Korps* and quickly turned the tables on the British, who up until then had been enjoying an almost unbroken run of success against the Italians. In April Yugoslavia and Greece were conquered, and in May Crete taken by German paratroopers, one of whom was the famous boxer Max Schemling who, finding parachuting "a great sport," clearly placed entertainment value above military expansion.

Hitler, fortified by these successes, promised his people an early end to the war through "victory in 1941" and prophesied that Churchill, rather than bring about the downfall of Germany, would, on the contrary, cause the destruction of Britain. On 4 May, at the conclusion of the Balkan Campaign, Hitler addressed the Reichstag again and denounced the British Prime Minister as the *Weltbrandstifter* (world fire-raiser). Seated on the government benches as usual was Rudolf Hess, Deputy Führer, and, after Goering, Führer designate. Less than a week later, on 10 May, under circumstances that, to this day, remain somewhat mysterious, Hess flew from Augsburg, in a specially adapted Messerschmitt Me 110, to Scotland allegedly in a vain attempt to bring about peace between Britain and Germany before the latter turned on Russia. The news that the nation's number three man had flown the nest was broken to the German public three days later when the papers of the Reich, with no variation whatsoever in the headlines, carried the same story:

> Rudolf Hess meets with accident. Party member Hess, because of an illness of many years' standing, which was becoming worse, and who had been forbidden by the Führer to do any flying, disobeyed this order and obtained a plane. On Saturday May 10 at six o'clock, he left Augsburg in the plane and has not been heard from since. A letter which he left behind shows from its confusedness the unfortunate traces of a mental derangement and one may fear that Party member Hess has been a sacrifice to a fixed idea. Hitler has ordered the immediate arrest of Hess's adjutants, who alone knew of the flight and of the fact that such flights had been

forbidden by the Führer, but who nevertheless did not prevent it, nor report it at once. Because of the facts, the National Socialist movement must unfortunately conclude that Party member Hess somewhere on his trip crashed and probably perished.

''All Germany'' observed a foreign correspondent, ''official and private, was in excited confusion''. Another official statement, again carried under identical headlines throughout the press, claimed that Hess

> lived in a state of hallucination, as a result of which he felt that by getting in touch with some English people . . . he could bring about an understanding between England and Germany. . . . The National Socialist Party regrets that this idealist fell sacrifice to his hallucinations. This, however, has no effect on the continuance of the war forced upon Germany. The war will be carried on until, as the Führer in his last speech said, the British rulers fall or are ready for peace.

Hess's flight was the number one topic of conversation throughout the Reich, and the Deputy Führer, previously one of the more popular of the Nazi leaders, became the butt of the latest *Witze* (jokes): the town's slogan took on a new meaning: ''Augsburg, Stadt des deutschen Aufstiegs''—''Augsburg, town of German ascent.'' There were mock radio reports: ''BBC: 'Weitere Einflüge von deutschen Staatsministern fanden in der Nacht zum Sonntag nicht mehr statt'''—''On Saturday night there were no further German cabinet ministers arriving by air.'' And spoof Forces announcements: ''Oberkommando der Wehrmacht Bericht: 'Goering und Goebbels sind noch fest in deutscher Hand'''—''German High Command Communiqué: 'Goering and Goebbels are still firmly in German hands!''' Finally, jokes concerning the sanity of the government were rife: ''Det unsere Regierung verrückt ist, det wissen wir schon lange, aber det sie es zugibt, det is neu!''—''That our government is mad, is something we have known for a long time; but that they admit it, *that* is something new!'' ''Churchill fragt Hess: 'Sie sind also der Verrückte?'—'Nein, nur der Stellvertreter'''—''Churchill asks Hess: 'So you are the madman?'—'No, only his deputy.'''

Baroness Agathe Fürstenberg-Herdringen, a member of the old aristocracy, renowned for her snobbery and wit, and who regarded all Nazis as parvenus commented, ''Wenn es so weiter geht, sind wir bald wieder unter uns''—''Well, if this keeps up we will soon be back among our cosy selves.'' Even in Nazi circles Hess had for some time been treated as a somewhat comic character; Goebbels regaled his staff on 21 May 1941 how when Hess's son was born all the Gauleiter (Party district leaders) were ordered to send bags of German soil from each *Gau* (district) to the Führer's Deputy. This soil was then spread under a specially-built cradle so that the young Hess could start life symbolically on German soil. Goebbels claimed that he himself—as Gauleiter of Berlin—had seriously considered whether it would be more appropriate to send a Berlin pavement stone. In the end Goebbels' gardener brought him a little heap from the manure bed which he duly dispatched in a sealed official package.

Goebbels himself, at this stage in the war by no means popular, was also the subject of many a witticism, albeit told with a cautious glance over the shoulder—a

*The front cover of the 1940 edition of* Der Angriff, *Goebbels' account of the Nazi ''struggle'' in Berlin during the late 1920s.* Der Angriff *was also the title of the newspaper founded on 4 July 1927, which was later to become the organ of Dr Ley's Labor Front.*

Kladderadatsch, *one of Germany's leading comic papers, of October 1941, shows "Roosevelt's dream"—the arrival of Josef Stalin and his gang in the White House following their flight from Russia ahead of victorious German Army. It was on 10 October 1941 that the* Völkischer Beobachter *claimed the "Campaign in East Decided!"*

glance that became known as *der deutsche Blick* (the German glance). Some played on his reputation as a ladies' man as when the Berlin *Siegessäule* (victory column), surmounted by a golden angel, was removed from its former location in front of the Reichstag building to a new home in the centre of the East-West Axis. Its height was increased by the construction of a new base, causing Berliners to quip: "Why did they have to put the angel up higher?"—"So Goebbels couldn't get at her." Other contemporary jokes reflected his unpopularity:

> Dr Goebbels was on the point of drowning in a lake when a young boy jumped in and saved him. Goebbels was not ungrateful. "How can I repay you, my young fellow?" he asked the boy.
> "Well, I think I would like to have a State funeral," the young boy answered.
> Goebbels was surprised. "At your age? Why, you're not going to die so soon."
> "Oh, no?" said the boy. "Just you wait till I get home and tell my father whom I saved from drowning!"

No sooner had the furore of the Hess affair died down than on 22 June 1941 Hitler turned eastwards and launched Operation Barbarossa against the Soviet Union. That morning's extra edition of the *Völkischer Beobachter*'s headlines screamed:

> War front from North Cape to Black Sea in bringing to reckoning of the Moscow Traitors. Two-faced Jewish-Bolshevik rulers in the Kremlin lengthen the war for the benefit of England.

Foreign observers noticed that for the first time since the war had begun, there was a momentary enthusiasm among the German people. It seemed that the war against Russia was the first popular campaign that had been launched. Few Germans had really been able to understand the reversal of policy in August 1939 when the Molotov-Ribbentrop Pact had been signed, for since 1933 the Soviets, along with the Jews, had been the objects of official denunciation. Now there was a sense of relief, "a feeling of final understanding." For the first time there seemed to be excitement about the war, and the belief that the "real enemy" was now being taken on was prevalent. This mood was not to last.

Soon German radio stations were broadcasting warnings of the danger of Soviet parachute troops:

> They may land in civilian clothes or come in the guise of farmers and try to carry out sabotage within the Reich . . . report the landing to the nearest police station or military post. . . . Be cool and don't spread false rumors.

The Soviet Embassy on Unter den Linden was closed and, as a cheap propaganda stunt, fumigated. The initial excitement died down very quickly, and soon Berliners were thronging to the Ruhleben racetrack for horseracing, the *Reichssportfeld* for a German championship football game and the banks of the Grünau for an international regatta. A neutral visiting the racetrack remarked on the quiet demeanor of the racegoers who commented among themselves on the progress of the race, but did not raise their voices. He was told by Guido Enderis, the head of the *New York Times* Berlin bureau: "They don't yell about anything anymore. Things are too serious for them these days." The seriousness of the situation was fully acknowledged in the press. On 3 August the *Völkisher Beobachter* stated "Every German citizen now knows the fight has been bloody and bitter. We have recognized that we are dealing with the most difficult enemy we have met so far." Goebbels' own paper *Das Reich* commented on the contrasts between 1914 and 1941:

> In the last war when there was a victory, flags were hung out and bells were rung without an order to do so. On the other hand, when there was a retreat, the people were just as depressed as they had been exultant after a triumph. In this war practically no feeling is shown, either in victory or when there is no news. In the last war there was something which could be called German feeling. In this there is only iron discipline.

An example of such iron discipline was witnessed by Harry W. Flannery, CBS correspondent:

> One day I was standing by a news-stand on the Kurfürstendamm when a woman approached the newsdealer to ask for change to use the near-by telephone booth. We noticed that she had a letter in her hand. She looked sad and worried. "Is everything all right, Frau Müller?" asked the newsdealer. The woman's expression was set. Her voice sounded hollow as she said: "No, I have just had bad news, and must phone my husband at work. You know we lost a son in Poland and another in France. Now I have word that Johann is gone too, our last son. He has been killed in Russia." The woman did not cry. She was too anguished for that. Her eyes were staring. We mumbled an attempt at commiseration.

Wounded soldiers and women in mourning, once fairly uncommon, were now seen daily on the streets of every town and city. And, on 1 September, another abhorrent feature appeared on German streets, for on that date it was decreed that all Jews over the age of six were to wear a yellow Star of David on the left breast with the word *Jude* in black letters to mark them out as the "racial enemy." When the Nazis came to power approximately 500,000 Jews (one per cent of the population) lived in Germany. Prior to the *Kristallnacht* pogrom of 10 November 1938 about 150,000 Jews had emigrated, and a further 100,000 left the Reich between *Kristallnacht* and the outbreak of war, whereupon the availability of transportation was severely limited. Jews, in relatively small numbers, were still able to emigrate until the autumn of 1941, but by then deportations to Poland had already taken place. Anti-Semitic "justification" of the introduction of the Yellow Star appeared in the *Völkischer Beobachter*:

> The German soldier has met in the Eastern campaign the Jew in his most disgusting, most gruesome form. This experience forces the German soldier and the German people to deprive the Jews of every means of camouflage at home.

As further back up, the Propaganda Ministry unearthed a book by an American Jew named Nathan Kaufmann, *Germany must Perish*, which called for the wholesale sterilization of the German people. Extracts were included in a pamphlet "The war aims of world plutocracy" which was first sold on news-stands for fifteen pfennigs, and then given away, one to each family in Germany, along with the monthly ration cards. The pamphlet ended with the following exhortation:

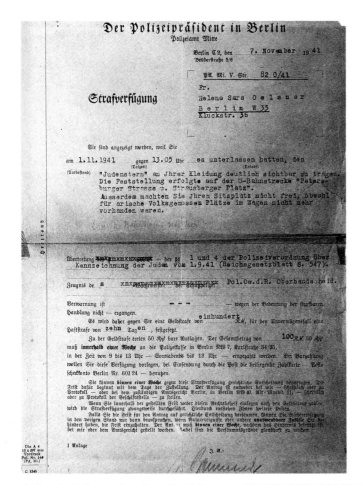

(Above) A charge sheet from Berlin's police records dated 7 November 1941 stipulates that Frau Helene Sara Oelsner is to pay a fine of 100 Reich Marks or face ten days in prison for not displaying her Jewish star in a prominent place where everyone could see it when she traveled on the U-bahn (subway) the previous week. Moreover she failed to give up her seat to Aryan passengers when the carriage was full.

(Above, right) A German Jew wearing the yellow Star of David, September 1941. A month after the introduction of the Star, deportations began to Polish ghettos. It is estimated that 170,000 German Jews perished in the death camps.

German people. You know now what your eternal enemy has prepared for you. There is but one means of frustrating these plans for our annihilation: Win. The reading of this Jewish murder-plan will steel your strength and make mighty your will to win. Now, go back to the gun, to the plough, and the lathe and the desk. The parole is Fight, Work, Win!

Its cover, jet-black with a bright yellow star, displayed the words: "Racial comrades. When you see this emblem, you see your Death enemy."

The new campaign was alleged by some to be a "monumental flop from the day of its birth," with many Germans asking one another why such a measure was necessary. Some reported an increase in incidents of kind acts to Jews. One story of the period was of the workman who got up and gave his seat in a tram to an elderly Jewess, wearing the Star. "Come on, have a sit down, my old starry doll" he said. When a Nazi Party member protested the workman simply said, "I'll do what I like with my own arse, if you don't mind." One of the American correspondents

> saw a big, fat, ill-tempered *Bürger* block with conspicuous intent the path of two SS men in uniform while an aged Jewess got out of a subway train first. One of the young SS men whispered something in the fat man's ear, but the man did not answer, and left them looking angrily at one another in the coach. I thought I saw the trace of a smile on the plump *Bürger's* face as he left the station.

Further justification of the Star's introduction was rooted in a whispering campaign which claimed that Roosevelt's administration had secretly adopted a law requiring all German-Americans to wear black swastikas on the left breast. The Yellow Star had thus been initiated, "reluctantly," by the Nazis as a sort of reprisal in an attempt to force the Jews of America to cease their persecution of Germans. Soon full-scale deportations began to major ghettos in the territory of the Government General (Poland), and also as far east as Minsk and Riga. By mid-1942 150,000 Jews from the "Greater German Reich" had been deported, 40,000 to the ghetto of Theresienstadt. This was supposedly the camp for "privileged" Jews, including those with high decorations won during the Great War. In reality it was a mere staging post to the gas chambers of Auschwitz.

While many Germans showed compassion for their Jewish neighbors' plight, others displayed attitudes of complete indifference. "Why should I care about the Jews?" one German asked Ursula von Kardoff, an anti-Nazi journalist on Berlin's leading daily the *Deutsche Allgemeine Zeitung*. "The only thing I care about is my brother, at Rshev (on the Eastern Front), and I couldn't care less about anything else." Concern for those on the Eastern Front increased with the failure of the Wehrmacht to achieve complete victory in Russia. As in 1940 spectacular victories had been won; 650,000 prisoners were taken at Kiev in September, but still the Russians remained unbeaten. Finally, on 6 December, with the spires of the Kremlin already visible to German troops, the Russian counter-attack began. The next day the Japanese attacked the U.S. Pacific Fleet at its base at Pearl Harbor, Hawaii; the "police action" against Poland had now become a World War.

On 11 December Hitler declared war on the United States in a speech full of coarse personal abuse directed against President Roosevelt. At the same time von

*(Opposite) In the same month that the Star of David was introduced for German Jews, an anti-Semitic exhibition* Le Juif et la France *was opened on 15 September 1941 in the Berlitz School building in Paris. Its express intention, encouraged by the German occupation authorities, was to show that "the Jews were responsible for the war and all of France's present misfortunes." 90,000 Jews from France, the majority foreign born, died as a result of the "Final Solution."*

*(Right) Champion skier Christel Cranz, winner of the gold medal for the women's combined downhill and slalom race at the 1936 Winter Olympics in Garmisch-Partenkirchen hands over her skis during the clothes collection 1941–42.*

*(Below) Nazi functionaries assist at a clothing collection during the early war years. The most famous of such collections took place in December–January 1941–42 and the last, the* Volksopfer *(the People's sacrifice), in January 1945.*

Ribbentrop handed Leland Morris, the U.S. Chargé d'Affaires, the declaration of war, whereupon Morris, his staff and the remaining fifteen U.S. correspondents were rounded up and interned at Bad Nauheim until the exchange for German diplomats from the Americas took place in May 1942.

Barely a week later, on 20 December, Goebbels addressed the people in a radio speech which "fell like a bombshell among the public." He announced that between 27 December and 4 January a gigantic collection of equipment for the Wehrmacht would be carried out. The Minister touched only lightly on the reasons for the collection. The Wehrmacht, he said, had made really big efforts to provide the soldiers with winter equipment. But winter had arrived earlier than anticipated and despite all efforts the equipment was still not secured. He finished with an urgent appeal to the solidarity of all Germans. A Swedish journalist, Arvid Fredborg, noticed that, despite sarcastic remarks as to whether it was not indeed reasonable to expect winter in December, the dominant feeling was that

> destiny's wing had touched the German nation in a way so far not experienced during the war, and that catastrophe was in the air. The prospect of the Russian masses welling over into Europe made even the most fanatical anti-Nazi prepared for sacrifice. The collection campaign actually produced a moral shake-up.

At the end of the collection it was stated that the Germans had voluntarily donated 1,500,000 furs and skins, and a further 67 million woollen garments. Prominence was given to film stars and other celebrities such as ski champion Christl Cranz handing over skis and clothes. Similarly, an old fur coat worn by Field-

*The Nazi ideal: an Aryan couple at the beach. "We demand of a member of this noble race that he marry only a blue-eyed, oval-faced, red-cheeked and thin-nosed blonde woman. We demand that he take as a wife a virgin only . . . We demand that the blue-eyed Aryan hero marry an Aryan girl who like himself is of pure and unblemished past."*
*From the Nazi weekly on "Racial Research."*

Marshal von Roon in the Franco-Prussian War of 1870–71 was photographed from the Eastern Front as an example of the virtues of both recycling and generosity. A *Deutsche Wochenschau* newsreel was shown of some of the 1,260 carriages filled with clothing setting out for the Eastern Front. No such publicity, however, was given to the confiscation of the Jews' winter furs, which also took place in January 1942. They had to be handed in with all labels revealing maker and owner removed.

The clothes collection, Hitler's sacking of the ''Eastern Marshals,'' von Rundstedt, von Leeb and von Bock, and the ''resignation'' of Army Commander-in-Chief Field-Marshal von Brauchitsch, together with America's entry in the war made for a gloomy New Year's Eve, 1941–42. A Swedish correspondent, Gunnar Pihl of the *Svenska Dagbladet*, recalled how in previous years,

> music streamed out from well-lighted, overcrowded restaurants. Cheerful, not altogether sober people danced ring-around-a-rosy around smiling policemen. . . . Since then an eternity had passed.

Now on 31 December 1941 Pihl saw

> no policemen, and hardly anybody else either. Somewhere on the Wittenbergplatz two youngsters, who were too young to understand . . . were bawling in the darkness. But otherwise I heard nothing but muffled sounds from some place on the Kurfürstendamm, perhaps from the Café Uhlandeck. There some dozens of Berliners were sitting and staring at one another over their beers.

To relieve such gloom an officially-inspired whispering campaign began with ''the coming spring offensive'' as its parole, and as early as 8 February 1942 the Home Front was assured that the worst was over. Hitler had taken over personal command after Brauchitsch's ''illness'' and ''resignation,'' and, according to an article entitled ''The winter passes'' in the *Münchner Neueste Nachrichten* of 8 February 1942, the troops of the Wehrmacht under his ''inspired leadership'' had won the great defensive battle in the East.

But winter had still not completely passed when Germany received heavy blows from the enemy in the West. On the 28 March the Royal Air Force made a devastating raid on Lübeck and a month later the 23 April saw the first of four equally devastating raids on Rostock. The Swedish paper *Svenska Dagbladet* reported that 3,000 houses in Lübeck were totally destroyed and on 4 April Gauleiter Kaufmann announced that

> endless caravans are speeding towards Lübeck with relief troops, food and material which are evidence of the dogged determination seen only in the German Reich.

The Propaganda Ministry announced that 295 people had perished in Lübeck, and on 7 April, to help the survivors,

> another large field kitchen has arrived in Lübeck capable of serving 25,000 meals a day. All the homeless who have relatives in the country are getting free railway tickets to go and stay with them.

Similar scenes were re-enacted in Rostock a month later where the authorities had to close the shattered town to all traffic. The *Hamburger Fremdenblatt* of 29 April warned its readers

*A small mobile soup kitchen established by the military authorities and manned by military staff.*

> it is entirely senseless to travel to Rostock because the inhabitants left long ago for places in Mecklenburg. Thus there is hardly any chance of finding relatives.

The period when the Nazis could still gloss over the effects of RAF raids and take parties of foreign correspondents to view bomb damage, (mainly churches and hospitals, of course), was definitely over. From Lübeck and Rostock onwards the Nazis were forced to admit the severe losses and destruction suffered by towns and cities in the north and west of Germany and furthermore acknowledge that this, coupled with a shortage of supplies, was having a detrimental effect upon morale. People accustomed to "butter with their eats" (see p. 147) did not welcome hardship. In an article entitled "Air attacks and the population" in the *Kieler Neueste Nachrichten* of 23 April appeared the following advice:

> The best shelter against air attacks is not concrete but a stony heart.

Yet many found the situation intolerable and took the opportunity, especially after the first "Thousand Bomber Raid" by the RAF on Cologne on the night of 30–31 May 1942, to "evacuate" themselves. The Swiss paper *Bund* of 13 July 1942 described the scene at Constance on the Swiss border:

> In spite of the warnings and difficult travel conditions, in spite of the appeals to refrain from making unnécessary trips, all hotels and boarding houses are crowded out. Most visitors come from places which have suffered air raids.

Despite reassurances on the radio on 7 May that night fighters were doing all they could to protect the population, the British bombers were getting through, and

Goebbels now started a ruthless propaganda campaign intended to stir the people back to a moral resistance and strength which had been previously torn down by earlier Nazi propaganda. After the Lübeck raid the Swiss radio commented:

> Since the Germans authorities have so far always tried to minimize the effects of the British attacks, this sudden change of policy [the publication of photographs showing the devastating results of the RAF raids] indicate that the destruction caused is so great that it can no longer be concealed.

Stories appeared that dealt with the heroism of civilians during the air attacks; the *Kölnische Zeitung* mentioned children fire-fighting after the "Thousand Bomber Raid," and earlier the *Essener Nationalzeitung* of 29 April had featured the story of the bravery of a boy of seventeen, who saved his father, caught in the debris of a house partly destroyed in an air raid. In true morale-boosting wartime spirit, the paper called upon the population not to shame themselves by letting boys teach them bravery.

Other youths earned no such praise. The middle years of the war saw a growth in the popularity of the "Swing Youth" movement; a movement consisting of teenagers from mainly middle-class families, who, in the words of an official report, favored chic-looking clothes.

> The predominant form of dress consisted of long, often checked English sports jackets, shoes with light crepe soles, showy scarves, Anthony Eden hats, an umbrella on the arm whatever the weather, and, as an insignia, a dress shirt button worn in the buttonhole, with a jewelled stone. The girls too favoured a long overflowing hairstyle. Their eyebrows were pencilled, they wore lipstick and their nails were lacquered. The bearing and behaviour of the members of the clique resembled their dress.

Swing Youth's favorite music was, as the name suggests, a blend of black jazz and white dance-band music of which Benny Goodman was the leading exponent. Indeed the Swing Youth movement used the greeting "Heil Benny" as well as cultivating a certain casualness (*Lässigkeit*) and sleaziness (*Lottem*). A member of a Kiel Swing Club, the "Plutocrats" (a favorite Nazi term of abuse for the British), summed up the philosophy and image of the movement in a letter to a friend:

> Be a proper spokesman for Kiel, won't you?—ie, make sure you're really casual, singing or whistling English hits all the time, absolutely smashed and always surrounded by really amazing women.

Naturally , the Nazis strongly disapproved of jazz and swing on account of their negro origins; the "Lambeth Walk" met with similar disapproval and was described as "a disgusting piece of Jewish apery." The Security Service of the SS gave the following report on a swing concert at the Caricata Bar, Hamburg in August 1942:

> The band played primarily German hits, but in a heavily "jitterbugged" style. . . . The applause after . . . English hits was extraordinarily loud and was in sharp contrast to the applause bestowed on the German numbers. Among other items the English hit "Sweet Sue" was performed, using the words "Lest das Mittagsblatt, lest das Tageblatt" [Read the midday paper, read the daily paper]. Since the "Swing Youth" have always sung the words in an amended form, "Lest das Mittagsblatt, lest das Tageblatt, alles

Lüge, alles Dreck, [. . . all lies, all rubbish], and as that is how they are
always known, this piece reaped particularly loud applause."

Himmler now busied himself with suitable punishments for these "teenage
rebels," and soon the public was reading of cases like that of Hasso Schutzendorff
who in October 1942 took his case to the Hanseatic Juvenile Court. The Gestapo had
put him in a concentration camp on the suspicion of being a Swing Youth. There he
had his hair shorn, was thrashed with an iron bar and forced to push earth-laden
trolleys uphill for a fortnight. The court's medical expert certified that Schutzendorff was suffering from general debility and exhaustion but the outcome of the case
is unknown. A much harsher fate than Schutzendorff's was reserved for the so-
called "Edelweiss Pirates" from Cologne, youthful working-class opponents of the
regime. In 1944, as well as sheltering Wehrmacht deserters, concentration camp
escapees and foreign laborers on the run, they made armed raids on military depots
and attacks on Nazi officials among whom was numbered as a prize victim the head
of the Cologne Gestapo. Soon afterwards caught by the Gestapo, their ringleaders,
including 16-year-old Barthel Schink, were publicly hanged in November 1944.

With fathers serving in the Wehrmacht and mothers coping with the everyday
difficulties of life on the Home Front, parental control was severely weakened
during the war years leading to an overall decline in moral standards and a greater
amount of undisciplined freedom for the younger generation or, in official Nazi
parlance, "juvenile demoralization." A report made by the provincial court at
Munich remarked that laxity of both outlook and behavior was becoming
particularly marked among girls. From the age of fourteen onwards, many of them
were unhesitatingly having sex with members of the Wehrmacht and the
*Reichsarbeitsdienst* (the Labor Service). After Hitler Youth parades, youngsters
roamed the blacked-out streets, went to films for "adults only" and generally fell
prey to adult "corruption." Cases taken at random from the records of a juvenile
court featured the following: three boys and three girls, all aged thirteen, who met to
engage in group sex; two boys, aged thirteen and sixteen, procuring three nine-
year-old girls for the same purpose; a sixteen-year-old boy hiring himself out as a
male prostitute; some fifteen- and sixteen-year-old girls engaging in "unnatural
sexual intercourse" with French prisoners of war; schoolgirls "ignorant enough of
their racial merits to accept payment in small change" for sexual favors; and finally,
a fifteen-year-old girl reproached by her mother for persistently hanging around SS
men and soldiers had allegedly been unmoved by the complaint, believing that if
she had got herself pregnant she would be just what the Führer was always asking
for—a German mother.

At the same time these cases were being heard the morals of the older generation
were under discussion by the Reich's top men. Goebbels recorded in his diary on 23
May 1942:

> I had a telephone conversation with the Reichsmarschall [Goering]. He
> complained about OKW's [the Armed Forces High Command's] protest
> against the new Leander film; this shows an airman spending the night
> with a famous singer. The OKW considers itself insulted morally and insists
> that a Luftwaffe lieutenant wouldn't act in that way. Goering, on the other

*Germany, the Axis allies and Axis- occupied territory.*

*(Opposite, top)* *Heinz Rühmann (right) in a still from* Der Gasmann *a comedy which, according to Goebbels' diary entry of 21 February 1941, made Goering laugh himself sick. It was premiered at the Ufapalast am Zoo on 15 February 1941. Goebbels himself thought it "drags a little in parts unfortunately. But otherwise a great artistic achievement."*

*(Opposite, left)* *Anny Ondra, wife of champion boxer Max Schemling and Heinz Rühmann's co-star in* Der Gasmann. *Correspondent Howard K. Smith recorded how* Der Gasmann, *which he described as a "second rate comedy" played "to packed houses at every presentation" at the Gloriapalast on the Kurfürstendamm while "fifty yards away at the Ufapalast an extra, super colossal one hundred and fifty per cent war film* Bomber Wing Lutzow *... showed to a half-empty theatre."*

*(Opposite, right)* *Willi Forst, one of Germany's leading actors and directors, whose great pre-war success was* Bel Ami. *Forst was Goebbels' first choice to play the title role in the anti-Semitic* Jud Süss, *a role which eventually went to Ferdinand Marian. Forst's biggest wartime film was* Wiener Blut *starring Willy Fritsch.*

*(Right)* *Paul Horbiger and Zarah Leander in a still from the most popular of all wartime films* Die Grosse Liebe. *Released on 12 June 1942 it was designed to show how "every war has a profound effect on human affairs." Because the propaganda content was minimal, the film was re-released after the war with an introductory paragraph inserted explaining that "the time in which it was made necessitated some slight military sentiments which could now be ignored."*

hand, correctly considers that if a Luftwaffe lieutenant didn't make use of such an opportunity he wouldn't be a Luftwaffe lieutenant.

The film under discussion was *Die Grosse Liebe* (The Great Love), starring the Swedish actress and singer Zarah Leander, and was described officially as showing how "every war has a profound effect on human affairs." The film contained characteristic wartime motifs and told of a famous Scandinavian singer who, through her love for a Luftwaffe lieutenant appreciates what it is to be a German soldier's wife. In the style of a true wartime heroine, she takes on an active role in the air raid shelter and in the life of the local community, and ends up singing for wounded German troops in Paris. The lieutenant, whose sense of duty, naturally, is stronger than his love, is contrasted with a composer, a rival for the singer's affections with the very un-German name of Ruchnitsky. When the war comes the latter can only think of his love for the singer, and is thus unworthy of her. Two songs from the film "Ich weiss, es wird einmal ein Wunder gescheh'n" (I know there'll be a miracle) and "Davon geht die Welt nicht unter," (The world's not going to end because of this) became tremendous popular hits at the time.

Zarah Leander had made a spectacular debut in German films on 31 August 1937 when she appeared in *Zu neuen Ufern* based on the story of an English singer, Gloria Vane; at the premiere in Berlin there were 78 curtain calls. From then on her career as a "substitute Marlene Dietrich" was assured and she became the leading female film star of the Third Reich, but, as a fellow Swede noted:

> I approve of Zarah Leander as a countryman: she is as Swedish and patriotic as her old tennis-playing king. She is more photogenic that he is, and was

Heinz Rühmann in: DER GASMANN

*Willy Fritsch (left) in the first German color feature film* Frauen sind doch bessere Diplomaten *(Women are better diplomats) in which he co-starred with Marika Rokk. It took seven million marks at the box office, and was given the state category of "popularly distinguished," although Goebbels at a private screening had lambasted the film and ordered: "take this rubbish out of my screening room and burn it."*

always wittily and adroitly defending the Swedish standpoint against German attacks. Why, then, did she appear in German films? The question is answered by reference to her popularity. She saw no reason to dispense with the millions the Germans dispensed to her.

On 1 March 1943, in the first of the large RAF attacks on Berlin, her villa in the suburb of Dahlem was hit by a bomb, and she barely escaped with her life. Prudently she returned to Sweden, after, it was rumored, throwing items from her extensive wardrobe to passers-by.

If *Die Grosse Liebe* was the most popular of the wartime films, taking 8 million marks at the box office, it was closely followed by *Wunschkonzert* (Request Concert), named after Germany's most popular radio programme which was broadcast every Sunday afternoon from 4 pm to 6 pm and which united Front and homeland under the direction of compère Heinz Goedecke. The story tells of two lovers who meet at the 1936 Olympics, lose touch, and are then reunited by means of the *Wunschkonzert*. The film, featuring many big names of the time (Wilhelm Strienz, Marika Rokk, Ferdl Weiss, Heinz Rühmann) was released on 30 December 1940, and took 7.6 million marks at the box office.

Another successful film was *Frauen sind doch bessere Diplomaten* (Women make better diplomats) which was Germany's first color feature film and starred Marika

Rokk with the debonair Willy Fritsch as her leading man. Willi Forst's *Wiener Blut* (Viennese Blood) was another successful film netting over seven million marks, but it was a film made just before the war, *Bel Ami*, that gave him his biggest popular hit, a song that went on to become famous throughout Nazi-occupied Europe:

> You're not virile, but charming
> You're not clever, but gallant
> You're the type of hero I like best Bel Ami

Other popular entertainers of the time included Johannes Heesters, described as "Germany's Maurice Chevalier," whose biggest successes were in films such as *Karneval der Liebe* (Carnival of Love), *Gasparone*, *Liebesschule* (Love School), and the operetta *Hochzeitsnacht im Paradies* (Wedding Night in Paradise); Grete Weiser, a leading comedienne; Ilse Werner, a Leander rival, and Evelyn Kunneke, whose biggest hit was "Sing Nachtigall, Sing" (Sing Nightingale Sing). Two of the most popular songs of the 1941–42 period were sung by Lale Andersen. The first, recorded before the war in Cologne in 1939, became the most famous song of the Second World War, sung not only in Germany but throughout the Allied camp as well. "Lili Marleen," based on a poem by a First World War minor poet Hans Leip, with music by Norbert Schultze, was broadcast over Radio Belgrade on the German forces wavelength to Rommel's *Afrika Korps* early in the summer of 1941. It soon became an established hit with Rommel's men, their Italian allies, and their British enemies. As with "Bel Ami" it became a hit throughout Occupied Europe, and Lale Andersen, until then an unknown cabaret *Chanteuse*, achieved superstar status. "Lili Marleen" was followed by "Es geht alles vorüber, as geht alles vorbei" (Everything passes, everything goes):

> . . . Erst kommt Dezember
> und danach der Mai
>
> (First comes December
> followed by May)

which was later parodied:

> Denn erst geht der Adolf
> Und dann die Partei
>
> (First goes Adolf
> And then the Party).

The parody eventually led to the song being forbidden in Germany and "excommunicated from the radio;" a radio which now in the winter of 1942 broadcast appeals to German women to give their bridal veils for mosquito nets for the *Afrika Korps*; a radio which now broadcast somber news of the Sixth Army at Stalingrad, the city which, in his speech at Munich on 9 November, the Führer had declared as good as taken. On Christmas Eve 1942 the German press stated: "The warriors at Stalingrad have been singled out by fate to give proof of Germany's honor and courage." All Germany braced itself for the inevitable.

*A beflagged Segringerstrasse in the small town of Dinkelsduhl in Bavaria. Hitler wrote in* Mein Kampf *of the red and white banner with the black swastika: "A symbol it really is! In red we see the social idea of the movement, in white the nationalist idea, in the swastika the mission of the struggle for the victory of the Aryan man."*

*(Above)  Two women using a mobile post office after the local post office itself has been destroyed by the Allies.*

*(Above, right)  The cover of the magazine* Die neue linie *of January 1942 featuring a picture of a sentry in the East dreaming of an idyllic homeland far away.*

*(Right)  Citizens in fancy dress collecting for the* Winterhilfe *fund-raising campaign.*

*(Right) A German railwayman decorates his locomotive with a "V" symbol. It was Victor de Lavelaye, head of the Belgian Service of the BBC, who first devised the idea of the "V" campaign to annoy the Germans in a broadcast to his countrymen on 14 February 1941. In retaliation, the Germans commandeered the symbol. "V" stood for Viktoria, it was claimed, an old Germanic word.*

*(Opposite) Breslau 1940: 5,000 Germans from the Baltic States and other parts of Eastern Europe are given citizenship by Himmler in his capacity as Reich Commissioner for the Strengthening of Germandom. Thousands of Poles were evicted from their homes to make room for these "colonists"—often at only a few hours' notice.*

*A group of elderly men and two women receive job instructions in an armaments factory.*

*An illustration from Kurt Ehrlich's 1942 book* Uniformen und Soldaten *showing the manufacture of Wehrmacht uniforms in a factory.*

(Above, right) A propaganda picture showing a female worker in a munitions factory.

(Above) A foreign female laborer at work in an armaments factory. By 31 May 1944, 5,300,000 foreign civilians and 1,830,000 prisoners of war were employed in German industry and agriculture.

(Right) Axis cultural solidarity: the Italian Air Force orchestra on tour in Germany in 1942 plays at a concert in a factory during the workers' lunch-break.

Nummer 32  SONNABEND, 9. AUGUST    23. JAHRGANG 1941  Preis 20 Pfennig

# Hamburger Illustrierte

**Ein Stuhl bleibt leer**
wenn der Frontsoldat ferngetraut wird.
Ein Rosenstrauß für die Braut liegt darauf
Aufnahme: PK. Böhmer (Weltbild)

*(Right) Posters of the* Reichskolonialbund *calling for the return of Germany's pre-First World War colonies in Africa.*
''*Germans have relinquished the thought of expansion beyond the seas.*''
 *Adolf Hitler, 5 May 1933.*
''*The claim to colonies will never more be silenced.*''
 *Adolf Hitler, 9 September 1936.*

*(Opposite) The cover of the* Hamburger Illustrierte, *9 August 1941, showing a wedding at the Front, attended only by the groom. The bride is represented by a garland of roses.*

*(Below) Released on 28 February 1941 and directed by Hans Bertram,* Kampfgeschwader Lutzow *was another film about the Polish campaign.*

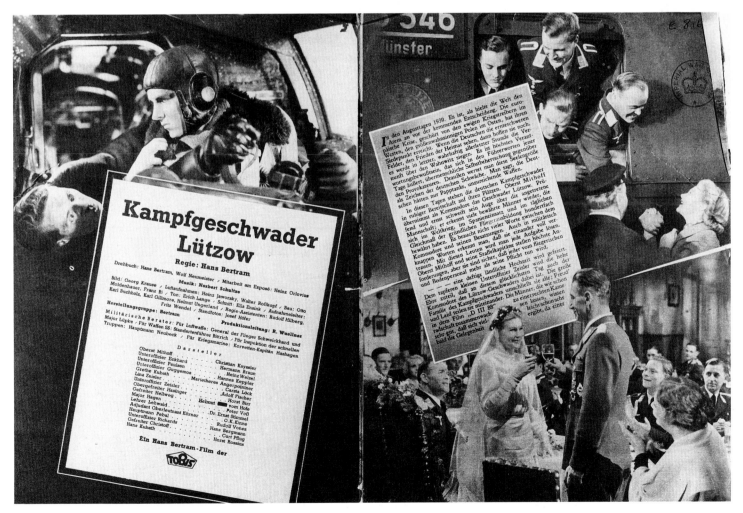

(Right) A German girl helps with harvesting the wheat during the early war years. A similar farmworker, Marianne Gartner, recalled her experiences on the land: "I received an official letter from the Kreisleitung (regional Party headquarters). It stressed the great war effort and the individual's part in the country's total commitment, and it contained instructions on where and when I was to report for a six-week service start on a farm where, together with another Primanerin (High School student), I was to look after small children, make myself useful in the house and help bring in the harvest."

(Below) German soldiers assisting farmers with the 1940 harvest. Just before the war Reich Minister of Food and Agriculture Walther Darre had admitted that there were 400,000 fewer workers on the land than when the Nazis had come to power. Throughout the war attempts to amend this situation were made by the employment of large numbers of prisoners of war, especially Frenchmen and Poles.

(Left) Soldaten von Morgen (Soldiers of Tomorrow) was the title of a 1941 film depicting the sterling military qualities of the Hitler Youth. Here a group are instructed in battle communications.

*The* Koloniale Frauenschule *at Rendsburg, was founded in 1926 under the joint aegis of the Reich Ministries of the Interior and Education. Girls were trained for life in the pre-1914 German colonies of the Cameroons, German South West Africa, German East Africa and Togoland, through a curriculum ranging from midwifery to winemaking, and from cobbling to ''Rassenkunde'' (raciology). It was not until the defeat at Stalingrad that colonial preparations and public agitation for colonies came to an abrupt end.*

*(Right)  A shooting party leaving for target practice.*

*(Below)  Physical exercise at the Colonial School.*

(Right) A six-week period is spent learning to run a household on a tight budget, attending a course on etiquette, and perfecting the social graces.

(Above) Learning Swahili for colonial life abroad.

(Left) A course in shoe repairing for future farmers' wives.

*(Opposite)  A beflagged village in the Bavarian Alps.*

*(Right)  A propaganda picture of a family group which appeared in* Ich Kämpfe, *produced by the Cultural Office of the Nazi Party, in 1942.*

*(Below)  A fashion feature from* Die neue linie *magazine advertising "sporty fashions" for the summer of 1942.*

die neue MODE-linie Juli 1942

(Right) In an attempt to disguise vital installations from the air many buildings throughout the Reich were covered with huge colored nets. The building shown is the Exhibition Hall on Berlin's Kaiserdamm shrouded in green netting to deceive the RAF and USAAF into thinking they were flying over a meadow. Similarly the Lietzen Lake in the industrial district of Charlottenburg was transformed to give the effect of a suburban landscape.

(Below) The slogan "No place like home" on the rucksack of a young evacuee. Following the massive RAF raids on Berlin in November 1943 when 992 bombers raided the capital, 400,000 Berliners were without shelter. Special evacuation trains were laid on but few chose to make use of them.

(Opposite) An aerial view of Cologne after the "Thousand Bomber Raid," 30 May 1942. It was estimated that 400 million cubic meters of rubble covered the devastated areas of Germany in 1945.

*(Right) German soldiers who had suffered arm wounds undergoing daily exercises with an expander. German military hospitals treated 52.4 million cases of sickness and injury between September 1939 and April 1945.*

*(Below) A BDM sports class.*

*(Opposite)* Ordensburgen *(Order Castles), the highest residential academies for the training of the Nazi élite. Hitler established three types of school for training future Party leaders: the* Adolf Hitler Schulen, *the Adolf Hitler Schools, closely associated with the Hitler Youth; the* Nationalpolitische Erziehungsanstalten, *the National Political Training Institutes known as* NAPOLAs; *and the* Ordensburgen. *The last two were under the direct administration of the Nazi Party, and the latter formed a kind of Party ''university.'' The* Ordensburgen *were named after the medieval fortresses built by the Teutonic Knights and four were eventually established at Crossinsee (see here), Sonthofen, Vogelsang, and Marienburg. An* Ordensburg *accommodated 1000 students called Junkers, who attended all four in turn, staying a year in each. Emphasis was placed on physical fitness rather than mental prowess with live ammunition being used in military exercises.*

*(Right)* Luftwaffe officers discussing salvage operations.

*(Below)* Hitler declares war on the USA, 11 December 1941.

*(Right) A recruiting leaflet for the 12th SS Panzer Division Hitler Jugend showing two enthusiastic youngsters. The 12th SS Panzer Division had its baptism of fire during the Normandy campaign in June 1944 when it came up against Canadian troops.*

*30 September 1942 at the Berlin Sportspalast: the audience greets Hitler as he opens the 1942—43 Winter Relief campaign.*

(Above) German Red Cross sisters supply coffee to servicemen on their way back to the front. German trains in wartime had the slogan "Wheels must turn for victory" painted on engines and coaches.

(Right) After heavy air raids local transport services were often destroyed or severely disrupted. To keep vital services functioning buses were frequently drafted in from other cities. Here Cologne residents board a Berlin double-decker bus in July 1943. The slogan reads "Berlin smokes Juno," one of the most popular brands of cigarettes in the 30s and 40s and still manufactured today. Ironically July 1943 was the month in which standardized cigarettes were introduced in the Reich.

*(Right)* A troupe of dancers entertains members of the Wehrmacht at a forces concert. Such shows were popular during the war and did much to maintain morale.

*(Below)* Kranzler's on the Unter den Linden in Berlin, an early wartime photograph.

(Right) The "Army of the Spade" was the official nickname given to the Reichsarbeitsdienst, *the Reich Labor Service. An annual "class" of twenty-year-olds were called up to do labor service each year. It averaged an annual figure of 400,000 in about 2000 camps. Shown here are the sleeping quarters in the camp at Bad Flensburg in Silesia—a converted factory which had been aptly decorated. During the war the* Reichsarbeitsdienst *were used as labor battalions behind the front line.*

(Below) *Workers from the Labor Service setting off to dig ditches.*

The front cover of the July 1942 issue of Die neue linie, *a prestigious "Vogue" style magazine which dated from the Weimar years and dealt with the arts and fashion.*

# 1943–1944

*A girl leaves a simple but poignant message for absent relatives on the door of her bombed-out house: "We're alive."*

# "Total war"

**O**n 4 October 1942 Hermann Goering marked the annual Harvest Festival celebrations by giving a speech at the *Sportspalast* in which he claimed: The worst is over; things will improve for we possess the territories with the most fertile soil. We shall send our best agriculturists to follow the fighting troops; they will provide our troops and the homeland with the produce of the land . . . we have taken the best provinces from the Russians . . . I have seen how the people live in Holland, Belgium, France, Norway and Poland. And I have formed a great resolve: foremost in the feeding of the hungry come the German people . . . If there is any hunger, it will not be in Germany . . . All the German Armed Forces are being fed entirely by the conquered regions.

The Reichsmarschall went on to conjure up images of "eggs, butter and milk in quantities you cannot imagine" and promised them all "fine food for Christmas." And indeed State Secretary Herbert Backe of the Food Ministry did manage to produce extra rations for Christmas 1942: 8·5 oz (250 g) meat, 4·5 oz (125 g) fat, 2 oz (62 g) cheese, 1·8 oz (50 g) coffee, 1 lb (·5 kg) wheat flour, and 4 oz (125 g) boiled sweets. A bottle of spirits was also promised but failed to materialize for some months, and once again "Es geht alles vorüber" was parodied:

> . . . der Schnaps in Dezember
> der kommt erst im Mai
> (Schnaps for December
> doesn't arrive till May.)

Despite this ration increase, the Christmas season, with the shadow of Stalingrad hanging over the country, was stamped by a marked severity. The capital's places of entertainment were full of passing visitors, mainly men on leave, but many Berliners stayed at home to sleep for a day or two since longer leave was, as a rule, not given this Yuletide. The New Year was much the same as Christmas, but while at Christmas time official propaganda had been soft-pedalled, at New Year the Germans were practically drowned in proclamations. The Führer himself, in his order of the day to the Wehrmacht, declared that Roosevelt and Churchill had taught Germany to hate. Goering said that all Germans were hoping that 1943 would be the "year of victory and peace." Gauleiter Grohe told the population of his *Gau*, Cologne, somewhat ominously, that every German, man, woman and child, knew that Germany *must* win "since failing that, she would not be allowed to live." Nevertheless, as the SS newspaper *Das Schwarze Korps* pointed out in December, if Germans really wanted to win the war the "last" reserves must fall into line:

In spite of all, we still have one foot planted in the realm of peace. In total war there is only total victory. This war is not going to finish up as a shooting contest. It is being waged for our lives. We cannot win it 50 per cent, not even 75 per cent, but only 100 per cent.

Nonetheless, grumbling went on extensively, especially in the food queues. People had to be careful, particularly since the Gestapo would on occasion arrest one or other of the particularly outspoken ones as a warning. One woman, accused of making the following remark to her companion "Let's get rid of the blasted swine, I say, Frau Muller. Away with the whole damned lot of them—then things'll be all right," evaded conviction with the innocent and patriotic answer: "Yes, judge, I said it all right. But of whom is your honor thinking? I meant Churchill."

It was on Monday 1 February 1943 that the fall of Stalingrad was announced. The surrender of the Sixth Army had been preceded by a host of rumors since nearly everybody in Germany had some relative or other there. The capitulation was shortly after the tenth anniversary of Hitler's assumption of power, an extremely muted affair when the Führer had declined to speak. Goering was to be the principal speaker, making his speech at 11am on 30 January. This had to be postponed

*"Can Nazi ersatz win?" asked* Picture Post *of 30 March 1940, warning its readers: "Our leaders must not underestimate German skill and effort in developing substitutes. 'Ersatz' with us is a joke. But 'ersatz' supplies 45% of Germany's peace time oil needs."*

**GERMANY'S BID TO BEAT THE BLOCKADE:** *S.A. Men Round Up All Scrap Metal*
*Half an hour ago it was a household stove. In a month's time it will be part of a shell or a torpedo. For years before the war, Nazi Germany was collecting, storing war materials—and at the same time developing the use of substitutes.*

**AN EMPEROR**
*No rubbish now in Germany. Everything is made to serve for the war effort. Statues from the squares can be usefully melted down. Ordinary metal household goods are now made of German chemists, backed by German financiers, have orders to evolve substitute oil, rubber, textiles, leather, paper, even metal itself.*

**BOUND FOR THE SCRAP HEAP:** *A Bust of Kaiser Wilhelm II is Carried Off to Swell Germany's Armaments "ersatz," or substitutes.*

## CAN NAZI ERSATZ WIN?

Our leaders must not under-estimate German skill and effort in developing substitutes. "Ersatz" with us is a joke. But "ersatz" supplies 45 per cent of Germany's peace-time oil needs. It has other imposing achievements to its credit.

FOR the second time in twenty-five years we are fighting Germany with the weapon of the blockade. By withholding from her supplies of raw materials and foodstuffs, we hope to weaken her industrial position sufficiently to make it impossible for her to sustain the material losses of prolonged and intense fighting. The Nazis, of course, knew that this would be our intention if they should force a war upon us. They consequently made their preparations to meet the danger well in advance. From the moment that Hitler came into power, the achievement of economic self-sufficiency has been the very foundation of their policy.

Unfortunately, as in so many other respects, the world was inclined to minimise the Nazi effort at ersatz production. I remember a talk I had in the summer of 1934 with the then British Prime Minister, Ramsay MacDonald. He was quite convinced that once the world economic recovery got into its stride, it would quickly put an end to Germany's autarchy plans.

But the Nazis knew what they were doing. They knew that sooner or later their foreign policy would make a clash with Britain and France probable. They were not going to be caught unawares by the blockade. For three years they spent enormous sums of money on substitute research. Their inventors were given unlimited facilities to discover new, and to perfect existing, processes for the production of substitutes.

By October, 1936, they had made sufficient progress for General Goering to say: "It is now possible to leave the experimental stage and with force and energy to turn our discoveries into practical use. In the near future factories will grow up in which we shall produce rubber, textiles, petrol and soap from the proceeds of our own soil."

Goering did not promise too much. The factories did grow up and started operation. When war broke out last autumn, Germany had created a substitute industry of impressive size. Some of its products were of excellent quality; others, again, were poor as compared with the natural product.

The most important substitute from the point of view of Germany's ability to wage a modern war, undoubtedly is oil from coal. Germany before the war had a consumption of approximately six million tons of oil and its derivatives. Of that, some two million tons were obtained by synthetic processes (Fischer-Tropsch process and hydrogenation). The basic product is coal and lignite (brown coal), both of which are plentiful in Germany. Petrol and lubricants from coal are still slightly more expensive, but quite as good as the derivatives from mineral oil.

Potatoes, too, are made to serve Germany's engines of war. At the outbreak of war, about 150,000 tons of alcohol were distilled annually from potatoes, and admixed to petrol. Finally, benzole, a by-product of the production of coke, contributed another 600,000 tons to the domestic production of oil. Altogether about 45 per cent of Germany's oil consumption was met by synthetic processes—a very substantial achievement indeed.

Since the outbreak of war Germany's petrol consumption has been drastically reduced, as no cars and motor-cycles are allowed on the roads, except by special licence. Simultaneously, the construction of new synthetic oil plants has been accelerated, and if we take into account the 600,000 tons of mineral oil obtained from German wells, it is safe to say that at present Germany is very near achieving self-sufficiency in oil. The position would, of course, change radically once

*The Hitler Youth Makes a Door-to-Door Collection*
*Discarded tins and cans from the kitchen no longer go on the dust heap. The German housewives deliver them up to the boys of the Hitler Youth to be saved and used.*

because the RAF raided Berlin, and for a full hour the radio played military marches with the announcer interpolating with news of the postponement from time to time. It was twelve o'clock before Goering could make his speech in one of the halls of the Air Ministry. The Propaganda Minister was more astute. At the midday press conference it was suddenly announced that Goebbels' speech had been changed from 4 pm to 3 pm. Goebbels intended to escape the British by speaking one hour earlier than scheduled. He arrived at the *Sportspalast* half an hour late and wearing a leather coat of the type he had worn in the early years of the struggle for power. He then "gabbled through Hitler's proclamation as if he had been standing on a fakir's bed of nails," and read his own speech at top speed to beat the RAF, who appeared promptly at 4 o'clock. The gist of the Minister's speech was that from now on the German people must throw in everything for a victory and show themselves worthy of the soldiers at the front—to which a powerful voice from the audience that checked even the speaker in mid-oratory, shouted "It is high time." None of those present could doubt what that meant, least of all Goebbels, who was annoyed that Hitler had entrusted to Field-Marshal Keitel, Chief of the OKW, Martin Bormann, and Hans Lammers, the head of the Reich's civil service, the task of implementing "Total War." Goebbels was only to be an adviser, but as his press aide Dr Semler noticed on 29 January 1943:

> Goebbels is brooding over a daring plan. He will try and bring pressure to bear on Hitler by putting forward radical demands in a speech at the *Sportspalast*. The crowd will applaud wildly. In this way he may be able to face Hitler to put an end to half-measures. If his demands are not met, then the Government will be compromised. The Führer could not afford that at the moment.

Sure enough on 18 February 1943 Goebbels made the greatest speech of his career under the slogan "Total War—Shortest War." To a hand-picked audience including Knight's Cross winners, wounded servicemen and celebrities such as Heinrich George, one of Germany's leading stage and film stars, he asked ten questions all on the theme of the last one—"Do you want Total War?"—to which everyone enthusiastically cried "Ja." Ursula von Kardorff noted in her diary:

> It must have been like a madhouse . . . our reporter [from the *Deutsche Allgemeine Zeitung*], . . . a quiet thoughtful man and anti-Nazi, told us how the audience roared and ranted. But even he caught himself jumping to his feet and for two pins he would have shouted too. Then he sat down again, shamefacedly. He said that if Goebbels had asked, "Do you all want to die?" they would have shouted "Yes" just the same.

The same thought had occurred to Goebbels who, in a hoarse whisper, said to his intimates afterwards: "What unprecedented, nightmarish lunacy. If I had commanded them 'Go jump out of the window of your apartment,' they would have done it." Later when his guests had gone, Goebbels undressed and weighed himself. His oratory had cost him seven pounds. As a result of the speech, new, radical measures were put into operation.

These measures were wide-ranging: early-morning horse-riding in the Tiergarten was forbidden as Goebbels, always to the left of the Nazi Party, thought it an affront

*(Opposite) An experimental tank, the Panzer Pz III/IV, engaged in rescue work on Berlin's Württembergerallee after the 16 December 1943 raid. After earlier raids units had arrived from Potsdam to assist in salvage operations. Goebbels noted: "I saw to it that the tanks were withdrawn to the Berlin barracks . . . otherwise we would certainly have read in the enemy press the following day that the Nazis had had to call upon the Wehrmacht to protect themselves from the furious people."*

# STRICKEREI UND STOFF

DS 14802
92, 100 cm
Oberw.

DS 14804
92, 100 cm
Oberw.

Zeichnung: Kürschner

DK 14803
88, 96 cm Oberw.

DS 14801
88, 96 cm
Oberw.

to working people. In the same vein the best-known luxury restaurants were to be closed, among them, Horcher's, the Taverne, Zum Alten Schweden, the Neva-Grill, Peltzer's Atelier and the Tuskulum on the Kurfürstendamm. Hans-Georg von Studnitz, working in the Foreign Office press department noted:

> The civil population is responding very willingly to the appeal for a greater war effort. Everyone seems to be ready to do his utmost, provided he is convinced that the restrictions imposed on him really serve a useful purpose. The closing of restaurants and nightclubs is hardly regarded as a measure calculated to win the war. As a waiter said to me a few days ago—
> ''Do you think the Russians will halt because Horcher's has been closed?''

Horcher's, situated in the Lutherstrasse was the most exclusive restaurant in the capital, and Horcher was employed personally by Goering himself for dinners and receptions. Tables had to be booked days ahead and most were ''permanently occupied by government and other officials, predominantly from the Air Ministry, the aircraft industry, the diplomatic corps.'' Goering declared that Horcher's should not be affected by ''the crazy Goebbels measures'' whereupon the latter secretly organized a demonstration of ''popular indignation'' against the restaurant. One night three men hired by Goebbels' staff smashed the restaurant's windows with the result that two policemen were commissioned to protect it against ''the rage of the people.'' On 17 March Goebbels spoke with Goering and urged upon the Reichsmarschall the necessity of shutting the place, telling him of the window-smashing incident and reminding him that as Gauleiter of Berlin he had it in his power to close the restaurant. To this Goering replied that he would turn Horcher's into an exclusive club for senior officers of the Luftwaffe. Goebbels retired defeated, only to turn his attentions to attacking other targets: beauty parlors, couturiers and hairdressers. ''Better to wear patched clothes for a few years than to run around in rags for a few centuries'' was the slogan of this campaign. Women did not need to dress up; they would please the ''victorious homecoming soldiers just as much in patches.'' Hitler himself intervened on this issue, telling his propaganda minister: ''The moment one tries to lay a hand on a woman's beauty care, she becomes his enemy.'' Goebbels had to retreat, declaring ''Total war is no arena for the mob . . . there is no need for a young woman to make herself ugly.''

Retired diplomat and anti-Nazi conspirator Ulrich von Hassell made further observations:

> The big speech by Goebbels reached a new pinnacle of filthy demagoguery directed against the upper class. Here is an example of the effect on imbeciles. The wife of Minister Thomsen [the German Minister to Sweden, Hans Thomsen, formerly Chargé d'Affaires in the USA] steps out of a subway. A man in uniform, heavy with braid—she thinks it was a police officer—storms up to her, snatches an ordinary, much-worn kid glove off her hand, and bellows: ''Haven't you heard that Goebbels has forbidden the wearing of kid gloves?'' A peroxide blonde passing by chimed in: ''Quite right.'' Incidentally, Goebbels had not said anything against kid gloves. But the stirring up of animosities and hatred is getting worse and what makes it still worse is that it originates in ''high places.''

*(Opposite) In the month that saw the nationwide clothes collection for the troops in Russia* Die neue linie *still featured in its January 1942 issue a fashion section ''Strickerei und Stoff''— on knitted and home-made fashion clothes for the more inventive. With Stalingrad and ''Total War'' measures* Die neue linie *ceased publication in March 1943.*

Other "Total War" measures included the curtailment of press reports on sporting events, and the stopping of professional sport altogether. From 1 March all periodicals which were not of importance to the war effort, including fashion journals, ceased publication. As von Studnitz noted "Their continued publication would be a farce anyway, seeing that there is hardly a stitch of clothing to be got anywhere."

Other measures included the closing of superfluous businesses, amongst them confectionery shops, the object being to release personnel for work of importance in the war industries. But, as a confectioner from Hanover told von Studnitz:

> The majority of sweetshops in Hanover are kept by little old ladies, who run tiny businesses in their own homes and with a minute turnover manage to make a minute profit. They are far too old and fragile to undertake any other sort of work; but their shops have been closed for all that, and the only one to suffer is the State, which has to assume responsibility not only for the board and lodging of these old ladies, but also for the interest on any debts they may have incurred.

Since 1939 a number of confectionery shops had been turned into grocery stores with sweets only representing a quarter of the stock. Nevertheless, the closure order was made applicable with effect from Spring 1939, and all shopkeepers who, at that time, were earning their living as confectioners, thus had to close. The net result was that a large number of general food stores had to cease trading. Such rigid adherence to "the regulations" caused much bitterness. One grocer named Schutte, reckoned to be one of the most efficient businessmen in the trade with a store on the Minsterplatz in Hanover, had to wind up his business and take on the job of liftman in one of the department stores.

Despite such regulations, quaint anomalies abounded in the spring of 1943. For a very long time, for instance, tiles for bathrooms had been unobtainable, yet almost every bookshop was full of tiles, bearing artistically painted slogans—such as "To each craftsman his own tools," "Don't fuss, man," "Don't worry, simply marvel," "Humor means laughing in spite of oneself"—which found a ready sale. Seemingly, no banality was too stupid to achieve immortality in the form of a painted tile, and a cartoonist pointed this up in a picture of a bathroom tiled solely with slogan tiles. But as von Studnitz commented on 14 April 1943: "the incidence of the almost pathological mania for slogans is one of the strangest phenomena of the war;" he cited some which appeared in public places:

> Tüchtiges Schaffen, das hält auf die Dauer kein Gegner aus
> (Strenuous endeavor will beat every opponent in the end)
> Alle Halbheit ist taub
> (Half-measures are no-measures)
> Was mich nicht umbringt, macht mich stärker
> (What can't kill me strengthens me)

In February excavations took place in Berlin's Pariserplatz and Wilhelmsplatz for the construction of air raid shelters. Control of the air was now almost totally in the hands of the Allies, and the Luftwaffe under Goering, moreover, was fast becoming

## WHAT HE EATS
### A Berlin Restaurant Menu: 1943

*Borchardt is a high-class restaurant in the centre of Berlin. This is a reproduction of an actual menu for March 4. It has one basic dish—red cabbage, potatoes and pieces of roast meat (kind unspecified). The soups are vegetable and "special." Or alternatively, there are "Field-kitchen dishes"—rissoles of barley meal and tomato for which the German has to give coupons for 150 grammes of bread and 5 of fat. The best dish is the last one—pork and Bavarian cabbage. The German does better with drinks. The wine list reads like a list of conquests beginning with Bordeaux. The cheapest wine has the general name "Foreign wine."*

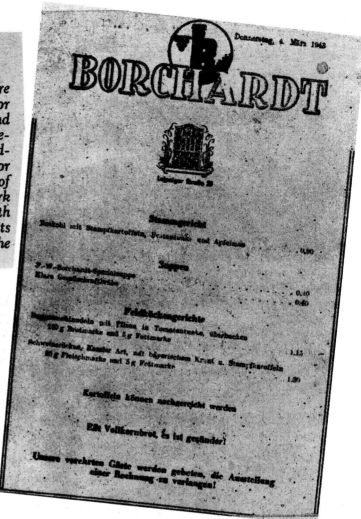

The menu of 4 March 1943 from Borchardt's restaurant, reproduced in Picture Post. *Above is the corresponding article.*

a discredited force. Berliners steeled themselves for the inevitable air attacks, which had already hit Cologne, Rostock and Lübeck. The first heavy attack took place on 1 March. Ulrich von Hassell described the night in his diary:

> First went to the theatre with the Waldersees to see a charming performance of "The Parasites," the closing words of which were superbly spoken by Walter Frank: "Justice exists only on stage." Frantic applause. Afterwards we had a very pleasant, leisurely meal at Borchardt's. But then hell broke loose! Very soon the neighbouring building began to burn; soldiers were called out of the shelter for rescue work; sparks rained down on the courtyard; and ashes began to drift in everywhere. . . . Finally, when the firing died down somewhat, Waldersee and I seized our wives and walked through the centre of the city, where fires were blazing in many places—Hedwig's Church, the arcade, about thirty roof fires in the Friedrichstrasse etc. An effort to reach the subway failed, so we went on foot through the Tiergarten, where we walked . . . on the wooded side. . . . We did not know that there were time bombs on the other side, one of which exploded the next day. Another lay for days at the entrance to the

*(Opposite) Shattered houses on the Tegelerweg, formerly a highly-populated residential area of Berlin, following the RAF raid of 3 September 1943.*

Bendlerstrasse. There were gruesome scenes also at the western end of town. . . . Many people are entirely or partly burned out. Almost all the buildings and collections in the Botanical Garden are destroyed.

Ursula von Kardorff wrote in her diary:

> A heavy raid yesterday. A roof was on fire near us, in the Augsburgstrasse. People formed a chain of buckets and Mamma and I helped. When we got home, rather exhausted, Papa met us in pyjamas, with a lighted candle in his hand, because there was no electricity, and Proust's *À la Recherche du Temps Perdu* under his arm. He simply could not understand why we had lent a hand. "Let the AGP get on with it," he said. He meant the Party [NSDAP], but he hates them so much that he deliberately refuses to mention the initials. I couldn't help laughing. Today we heard that 1,700 fires had been started and the Pragerplatz, quite close to us, is completely destroyed. The Raths lost everything they possessed including their photographs of their son Ernst [vom Rath, whose death led to *Kristallnacht*] . . . and of the son who was killed in the war. Everyone in Berlin is saying that the raid was a reprisal for the deportation of the Jews;

a view certainly shared by anti-Nazi Ruth Andreas-Friedrich:

> The English have avenged the monstrous dead with a shattering raid on Berlin, the like of which has never been seen. A hundred and sixty thousand are said to have been made homeless. The city and all the western and southern suburbs are on fire. The air is smoky, sulphur-yellow. Terrified people are stumbling through the streets with bundles, bags, household goods, tripping over fragments and ruins. They can't grasp it that they—they, in particular—should have been the ones to suffer so. From cause to effect is a long road. Very few people know enough to follow it. One hardly realizes that today's consequence may have been yesterday's cause. The cause of Coventry, the cause of Dunkirk, the cause of Jewish atrocities, of rubbing out cities, of concentration camps. The broom that is sweeping Germany Jew-free declines to go back to its corner. And the spirits that we have summoned up will not let us go.

The fresh round-up of Jews, designed to make Berlin *Judenfrei* (free of Jews) began on Sunday 28 February at six o'clock in the morning. In a number of places the SS men supervising the deportation met with hostility from the public. Ursula von Kardorff described the scene in her diary:

> . . . around the Rosenthalerplatz, working-class women had gathered and protested noisily against the deportation of the Jews. Armed SS men with fixed bayonets and steel helmets were dragging miserable figures out of houses. Old women, children and terrified men were loaded into lorries and driven away. The crowd shouted "Why don't you leave the old women alone? Why don't you go out to the front, where you belong?" In the end a fresh detachment of SS appeared and dispersed the crowd.

One of the victims was the widow of Max Liebermann, famous painter and president of the Prussian Academy of Art in the pre-Hitler era. She was eighty-five years of age and bed-ridden; when the SS arrived for her with a stretcher she took an

*(Opposite)* Technische Nothilfe *(emergency repairs and engineer troops) and Wehrmacht railway troops laying new track at Berlin-Wedding railway station, following damage sustained in an Allied air attack on 23 March 1944. Before 1933 Wedding had the reputation for being the most fiercely Communist district in the capital.*

overdose and died the next day in the Jewish Hospital without gaining consciousness. Arvid Fredborg, just before returning to Sweden, witnessing the following incident, noted a certain wariness of foreign publicity:

> I was on my way to the police station in Sächsischestrasse to report my departure when I noticed *die grüne Minna*—the feared Black Maria, which is green in Berlin—standing outside. Suddenly a very old woman was brought out of the station into the carriage. Her face was numb with fright. As the car started an elderly German woman rushed up to it and tried to open the door, but was hustled off. All the while she was shouting hysterically, ''But she is no Jewess—I've known her for thirty years, and I know that she is no Jewess.'' The car disappeared, and finally she went in to the officer I was on my way to see and beseeched him to save her friend, with whom she had been living for half a lifetime. ''I know that she is no Jewess,'' she sobbed, ''You must help me.'' The policeman squirmed, embarrassed, and tried to calm her down by telling her that nothing would happen to her departed friend. But the woman cried, ''I know what they do with the Jews.'' She was not to be pacified, and when the policeman discovered me, whom he recognized as a foreigner, he took her by the arm and led her out, telling her that she was lucky to have been spared from accompanying her friend. We stood there silent, the policeman and I, while he noted down my departure. When I was about to leave he said half to himself: ''*We* can't help it, you know.''

Officially, ''the Reich capital had stood up to the test'' of the 1 March raid; to bolster morale Goebbels, wearing a steel helmet, appeared on the Breitenbachplatz immediately after the bombing and distributed bars of chocolate to children. Nevertheless, there was a distinct atmosphere of discontent and one group of Nazi officials were greeted with an ironic chanting of the slogan ''We thank our Führer.''

Whilst Goebbels recognized that, as he put it, ''grumbling is the laxative of the soul,'' he also acknowledged that there was a need to improve home front morale. Consequently, a new campaign was arranged; as Gunnar Pihl put it, he

> organized one of the biggest curiosities he had ever officially staged, a competition in politeness for transport employees, waiters, store clerks, and officials of Berlin. The public wrote in and suggested people who were specially polite; the Minister of Propaganda distributed prizes, a thousand marks, a radio, and twenty theater tickets to the four politest ones. Politeness was filmed and shown on the movies. Polite people received a pin as a sign of their civility, a pin with the Berlin bear on it. When distributing the pins, Goebbels declared that the people of Berlin were fundamentally tremendously polite. Humorous and polite. Impoliteness was only an exception. . . . Ten days later he had thousands of posters printed which were set up everywhere. . . . Berliners must strive to be polite, he wrote. They must be polite, especially toward the sick, old people, and women.

The competition was a psychological blunder and had very little effect other than offending the Berliners' feeling of self respect. Certainly a few waiters were fired and

*''Yesterday I was in Cologne with Goebbels. I saw a heavily bombed city for the first time.... It is surprising that Goebbels was everywhere cordially greeted in the streets. He talked to the people in the Rhineland dialect. One sees even in Cologne that, at the moment, he is the most popular of the nation's leaders. These suffering men and women feel that at least one of them is interested in their fate.''*
*Dr Rudolf Semler, Goebbels' Press Officer, 10 July 1943.*

sent to do hard labor in a concentration camp to give the profession a fright, but, as rumors had it, the owner of a textile firm in Hamburg who had mistreated some teenage women workers was merely fined a 100 marks, a paltry sum to an industrial executive, but then, *he* was a Party man.

It was at this time that a spontaneous uprising against the Nazis took place in Germany. Ironically it happened in Munich, the ''Capital of the Movement.'' University students in Germany had been the most fanatical of Nazis in the early 1930s. Ten years of Nazi rule had brought disillusionment, sharpened by the failure to win the war, and the catastrophe of Stalingrad. Consequently, the University of Munich became a center of student unrest. The protest was led by Hans Scholl, a twenty-five-year-old medical student, and his twenty-one-year-old sister Sophie, who was studying biology. Professor of Philosophy Karl Huber was their mentor. By means of what became known as the ''White Rose Letters'' they carried out anti-Nazi propaganda in their own and other universities, and were in close contact with anti-Nazi groups in Berlin. One day in February, the Gauleiter of Bavaria Paul Giesler, having seen the Gestapo's file of ''White Rose Letters,'' convoked the student body and announced that the physically unfit males—the fit ones were all in the Wehrmacht—would be directed to some kind of war work. He then, ''with a leer,'' suggested that the female students bear a child each year ''for Führer and Fatherland,'' adding that if any of them lacked sufficient charm to find a mate, he would assign to each of them one of his adjutants, and furthermore promise them a ''thoroughly enjoyable experience.'' Although Bavarians are noted for their robust sense of humor, this coarseness was too much for the students, who proceeded to shout Giesler down and throw his SS escort out of the hall. That afternoon they spilled onto the streets of Munich demonstrating against the regime; the Scholls distributed leaflets calling on German youth to rise up against Hitler. On 19 February they were seen throwing leaflets from the balcony of the university and betrayed to the authorities. Brought before the president of the People's Court, ex-Communist turned rabid Nazi, Roland Freisler, they were found guilty of treason and sentenced to death. Sophie Scholl had been badly hurt during interrogation by the Gestapo and appeared in court with a broken leg, but nevertheless put up a spirited resistance to Freisler's cross-examination. She went to the scaffold on her crutches and was beheaded by a public axeman grotesquely attired in formal evening dress of top hat, white tie and tails, dying, as did her brother, Professor Huber and other students "with sublime courage."

The summer brought the fall of Mussolini on 25 July 1943 and, on the same day, a devastating air attack on Hamburg. Whole sections were wiped out in the fire storm and about 75 per cent of the city housing a million inhabitants was destroyed; 30,000 were killed. For weeks eyewitnesses were unable to report without breaking down and weeping hysterically. Survivors poured out of the city in wild panic trying to get as far as possible from the place of horror. And among the refugees were many who, according to government instructions, should have remained in the city; German and foreign workers alike had "flung duty to the wind." After the initial attack, arrangements to feed and shelter the bombed-out functioned for three days only before failing completely.

For a time, the vital contribution to the war effort made by Hamburg's shipbuilding yards and large armaments factories was brought to a complete standstill. To get life going again, officials who had fled in panic were ordered under threat of heavy penalties to return. In the first half of August, official appeals were

*A Hamburg street scene after the raids of July–August 1943.*

published in the newspapers of the provinces around Hamburg requiring fugitive policemen, railwaymen, local government officials and other civil servants to report at once to their posts. The propaganda apparatus referred to these raids as "terror attacks" and to the British and American airmen as "air gangsters" or "air pirates," who dropped bombs only when they could be sure of hitting dwellings, killing women and children, or destroying hospitals, churches and other "cultural objectives." Guernica, Warsaw, Rotterdam, Coventry and Belgrade were conveniently forgotten. Dr Ley, Housing Commissioner and head of the Labor Front, announced in *Der Angriff* of 4 July that enemy air raids had devastated a million apartments up to that time. On 30 October he stated that the number had risen to 2 million. A special decree of 16 July permitted workers who had been bombed out to absent themselves from work for at least a fortnight and granted them 90 per cent of their wages for that period, provided their places of work were intact. And indeed, most industrial plants made a speedy recovery; Muthesius, economics editor of the *Deutsche Allgemeine Zeitung* wrote in August 1943:

> Often one hears that this or that factory or this or that assembly plant was completely devastated, absolutely finished. And then, a few days or a few weeks later, the plant still worked. The people got out from under, readjusted, rebuilt, repaired. . . . Though it would be stupid to minimize the difficulties, one thing is undeniable: our experience thus far testifies that our capacity to produce cannot be completely strangled by the air terror.

That summer further strenuous efforts were made to stiffen morale. Newspapers protested against defeatism especially in view of the now widely-held feeling that: "It can't get worse than it is now: even after a lost war our lives cannot be worse than now." Gauleiter Hoffmann comforted the bombed-out people of Bochum by telling them that the Führer had enquired after their fate by telephone immediately after an air raid. In heavily-raided areas indoctrinating posters declaring "Have confidence in the Führer," and "The Führer is always right" were displayed. Anti-Nazis over-printed or added their own slogans such as "The whole mess is the Führer's fault," for instance, or "Put an end to the war," "We have had enough of war."

The nerves and spirits of the air raid victims were further adversely affected by red tape and disputes over securing compensation for losses, which should automatically have been their lawful due. A distinction was made between damage to be compensated immediately and damage "that cannot presently be requited because of the absence of commodities." For immediate compensation, in the case of damage to essential clothing and indispensable household goods for example, the victim received either merchandise or the money equivalent. For whatever could not be replaced, the claimant received a credit note which was not negotiable until the goods in question became available—that is, until after the war. Many claimed that they were unjustly treated, but there were also frequent newspaper reports of people sentenced to prison, and even to death, because of alleged improper claims for damages. Looting was also punishable by death, as were certain types of "blackout crime," such as bag-snatching—for which three youths in Hanover received the death penalty as early as 24 October 1939.

The authorities insisted that citizens in parts not bombed, whose general living standards were, according to Goebbels, ''far higher than those in the air-war areas'' make sacrifices for those who had suddenly become dependent. Thus on 1 August 1943 clothing coupons were completely suspended, and whereas it had even before been impossible for a German to buy an overcoat or heavy outer-garment without a special permit, that permit was now only granted if the applicant could prove ''dire need.'' The suspension was alleviated on 5 November to the extent of allowing one pair of rayon socks or stockings to each adult card holder.

After the disaster of Hamburg, it was almost certain that Berlin would be the victim of similar devastating raids. Ruth Andreas-Friedrich recorded in her diary on 8 August that citizens were being advised to evacuate the capital:

> ''Men and women of Berlin'' a hoarse voice rattles out. ''The enemy is ruthlessly continuing his aerial terror against the German civilian population. It is urgently desired, and is in the interest of every individual who is not obligated for professional or other reasons to stay in Berlin— women, children, pensioners, and those who have retired from active life— that such persons move to regions less subject to air attack.''

A leaflet to this effect had already been put through all the city's letter boxes a week earlier. Heavy raids on the capital took place on 23–24 August, 31 August–1 September, 3–4 September, 8–9 October and 17–18 October, but it was not until the night of 22–23 November that the Battle of Berlin began in earnest. To Hans-Georg von Studnitz this raid ''seemed like the end of the world;'' Berlin had ''become one vast heap of rubble.'' In his diary he recorded the bizarre happenings attendant upon the raid. A tiger, which had escaped from Berlin Zoo was said to have made its way to the Café-Josty, gobbled up a *Bienenstich* pastry there and promptly dropped down dead. One person, who drew uncomplimentary conclusions from the event as to the quality of Josty's baking, was sued for libel by the Cafe's owner. The court ordered a post-mortem and found, much to Josty's satisfaction, that the tiger had died from glass splinters found in its stomach. Other rumors in circulation claimed that escaped crocodiles were to be found on the banks of the Landwehr Canal. Nearly all the major hotels, including the Eden, the scene of roof garden *thé dansants* before the war, had been wrecked. One of the exceptions was the Adlon Hotel, described as an ''oasis'' in the rubble, but even the Adlon, the premier hotel of the Third Reich, could only muster up cold cuts and potato salad for the Argentinian Chargé d'Affaires, Luis Luti and his wife, served in a single unheated room.

Two victims of the raid were Goebbels' mother and mother-in-law, who were bombed out completely in the Moabit district of the city. The Doctor, touring the city to see the vast extent of the damage, including the famous Romanisches Café and the Kaiser Wilhelm Memorial Church (which, to this day stands in its ruined state on the Kurfürstendamm as a monument to the horrors of war), was greeted by Berliners:

> I was amazed at their excellent spirit. Nobody is crying, nobody complaining . . . the morale shown here by the population of Berlin is simply magnificent.

*Nuns assist with salvage work following an air attack on Berlin, 1943.*

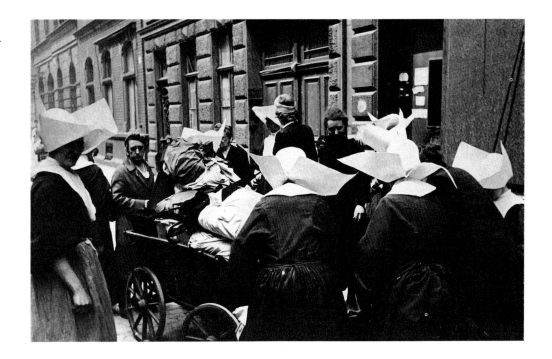

Throughout the winter of 1943–44 the bombers returned, yet life went on. Indeed, after the first November raid Ursula von Kardorff recorded in her diary: ''Everything goes on as usual at the office. Berlin is so large that some of my colleagues never even noticed the raid.'' She later observed a gang of Russian prisoners, ''looking like ragged wraiths,'' clearing up the debris, just a few of the many millions of foreign workers—some volunteers, the majority forced labor— now in the Reich. Whilst those from the west, France, Belgium, and Holland had a certain amount of freedom, workers from Poland, Russia and the Ukraine were, on official instructions, treated as serfs. Poles who had sexual relations with German women were shot or hanged, for instance, and any acts of kindness on the part of the Germans were harshly punished. A friend of the von Kardorff family who attended the funeral of a worker from the east on his own Pomeranian estate was arrested the next day and put into prison for six months.

Despite the ''Total War'' measures of the year before, at the beginning of 1944 luxury restaurants, such as the Neva-Grill on the Bayreutherstrasse, still functioned with their ''polite waiters, *hors d'œuvres*, fried fish and plenty to drink.'' Alternately people in the capital could find spiritual nourishment in concerts such as the one given by the Fehse Quartet in the half-gutted Philharmonic Hall on 19 February, when they played Schumann to an audience listening with ''dedicated attention.'' As the battle began to subside von Kardorff took stock:

> I feel a growing sense of wild vitality within myself, and of sorrow too. Is that what the British are trying to achieve by attacking civilians? At any rate they are not softening us up. . . . The disaster which hits Nazis and anti-Nazis alike is welding the people together. After every raid special rations are issued—cigarettes, coffee, meat. As Dostoevsky's Grand Inquisitor said, ''Give them bread and they will back you up.'' If the

*The Berlin Philharmonic, conducted by
Wilhelm Furtwangler, playing a
Beethoven concerto during the lunch
hour in a German armaments factory,
1944. The original wartime caption in
the propaganda magazine* Signal *read
''What we are fighting for: For man's
right to culture.''*

British think that they are going to undermine our morale they are barking up the wrong tree.

And the bombings produced their own brand of wry humor:

Wearily I go to bed
Bombs still falling round my head
O flak, now let thy watchful eyes
Guard us till the sun doth rise
O Father God, avert Thy gaze
From the havoc that the Tommies raise
With Thy help we'll not despair
And soon the damage will repair
Friends and neighbors, each must roam
Parted from his blazing home
Great and small must share the woe
Of ruins and no place to go
Shut little mouth, sink little head
Pray for final Victory instead
Help the farmer God, we plead
In his present need
Restore him to his portly frame
Let Goering once more be his name

was a ''prayer'' which children would recite before going to bed. Another mock ''grace'' finished thus:

> No butter with our eats
> Our pants have no seats
> Not even paper in the loo
> Yet, Führer—we follow you.

And von Studnitz recorded another piece of doggerel dealing with the theme of ''Total War'' which contained the following verses:

> Tramcar filled to bursting point
> With shoving, sweating, howling brutes
> Nothing in our butter-dishes
> No coal coming down our shutes.
>
> Houses without doors, roofs, windows
> The rain will wash us all away
> Men as thin and pale as ghosts
> Rations smaller every day.
>
> On a slightly bomb-struck sofa
> You stretch at ease and start to puff
> At a cabbage leaf whose rich aroma
> Fills the house—what curious stuff.
>
> Peace—then through the night air screams
> The siren's love song, peace to mock
> ''This bloody war will drive me barmy
> Must they *always* arrive at six o' clock?''
>
> Feeling gloomy, dearest friends?
> Why, our victory is sure.
> Over the slogan ''stick it out''
> Just write the headline ''Total War.''

To offset such expressions of ''defeatism,'' Party speakers from Goebbels downwards now spoke of retribution and ''wonder weapons,'' which would soon appear and be used against the Allies. Pathetic attempts were made to brighten up the ruins of Berlin and other bombed cities, especially on the Führer's fifty-fifth birthday, 20 April 1944: ''the streets have been brightened up in a rather hectic fashion,'' noted von Kardorff:

> Red flags wave from every empty window-frame. Some bold spirit even clambered up the front of the Bristol [Hotel], probably with the help of a fire ladder, and hung up an enormous flag. People were buried under those ruins and their knocking could be heard until they stifled to death. The heaps of rubble are gaily decorated with little paper flags, and streamers bear the words ''Führer, Command. We'll follow'' or ''Our walls are breaking, but not our hearts.''

*7 October 1943: the front cover of the Nazi Party's* Illustrierter Beobachter, *the illustrated weekly and companion to the daily* Völkischer Beobachter. *During the war there was a dramatic increase in circulation of such papers, the* Illustrierter Beobachter *and the* Berliner Illustrierte *gaining about nine million readers between 1939–44.*

*(Opposite) The* Illustrierter Film-Kurier *featuring an early wartime film* Das Gewehr über *(Shoulder Arms) which was released on 7 December 1939. Described as "a silly farce" it was banned by the Allied authorities after the war together with 20 other films out of the total of 118 produced that year.*

Silberne Nahkampfspange und zwei Panzervernichtungsabzeichen.
Dieser Unteroffizier aus Magdeburg ist im Zivilberuf Steinmetz; die Schläge, die er als Soldat austeilt, können natürlich nichts anderes sein als Hammerschläge, von denen jeder richtig sitzt.
PK.-Aufnahme: Kriegsberichter Scheerer (Scherl).

Illustrierter
Film-Kurier

Das
Gewehr
über

(Opposite)  The Berlin fire brigade at work, 1943. That autumn and winter fire brigades from as far away as Dresden were called to assist the capital's firefighters.

(Right)  This photograph appeared in the London News Chronicle of 31 January 1945 with the following caption: "The latest picture of Hitler to reach London last night.... Hitler sad-faced and in a sombre mood, hat in hand, is surveying ruins of a German town, the name of which is not disclosed." In fact the photograph was taken on a pre-war occasion as Hitler's uniform indicates—he stopped wearing the swastika armband on the first day of the war—and probably shows him surveying the damage caused by some domestic disaster such as a gas explosion or fire.

(Below)  A gang of voluntary workers pull down the unsafe walls of severely damaged houses.

*(Opposite)  A young boy makes sure his cat is safe in the chaos after a raid.*

*(Right)  A German soldier engaged in rescue work surveys the ruins of Berlin's Württembergerallee following a raid on 16 December 1943. Fifteen bodies were recovered from this house alone. A survivor described how twenty explosions were counted in as many minutes in the immediate vicinity of the trench in which he was forced to spend the night.*

*(Below)  Victims of the Berlin raid, December 1943, are laid out for identification in a gymnasium incongruously decorated with Christmas trees. In the last eighteen months of the war 77,750 German civilians reported missing throughout the Reich were never found.*

*(Right)  Foreign workers at a soup kitchen, 1943.*

*(Opposite)  An unsafe wall is removed from a derelict building, 1943.*

*(Below)  Two looters caught by the camera, early 1945.*

*(Above) Berliners wheeling salvaged possessions and furniture through the streets after losing their homes in an air raid.*

*(Opposite) A ruined street following an air attack. Some household goods have been salvaged, and the notice on the tree warns of severe penalties to be meted out to looters. In Berlin, on account of the thousands of foreign laborers, the red placards were printed in German, French, Russian and Polish.*

*(Right) A mother amuses her child whilst waiting for transport to a center for homeless and displaced persons.*

*(Right)* A woman, homeless after a bombing raid in 1943, sits amongst her salvaged furniture in the ruins of her house.

*(Opposite)* Identification of the dead following a raid.

*(Below)* Salvage work in Berlin, 1943.

(Above) Men from the Technische Nothilfe (emergency repairs and engineer troops), covering a "dud" bomb with bales of paper following an Allied air raid.

(Right) Special civil defence bicycle troops such as these were formed to assist with rescue and repair work.

(Opposite) Salvage troops setting off on bicycles to start rescue work and repairs following an air raid.

*(Opposite) Building extra housing for the homeless in the countryside.*

*(Right and below) By the beginning of 1944 Germany needed an estimated eleven million extra dwellings. Before the invasion of Russia in June 1941, the Reich had already been six million apartments short, but Allied bombing in the following years had caused a rapid escalation in the housing shortage. The desperate situation forced the government to build emergency accommodation for the bombed-out, a programme put into effect from 1943. The houses were simple, two-roomed constructions, made of wood and built on estate complexes. Inside, they were small but often very cosy.*

It is estimated that over 800,000 civilians were killed by bombing, 1939–1945. The RAF and USAAF dropped 2,697,473 tons of bombs, about 50% of which fell on residential areas, and only 12% on factories and war-connected industries. Over 3,600,000 homes were destroyed and 7,500,000 people were made homeless. Some 2,500,000 German children were evacuated in the course of the war. In all it is reckoned that 3,640,000 German civilians died as a result of Hitler's war.

(Opposite)  A woman washing up at one of the street water pumps.

(Right)  Homelessness brought with it an inevitable lack of privacy—a woman at her wardrobe one morning.

(Below)  Centers such as this one where people could buy, barter or exchange clothes were set up amidst the ruins.

(Above) An anti-Nazi satirical cartoon based on Hitler's quotation ''Where the German soldier stands, no one else gets in.'' Anti-Nazi papers such as Der Friedenskämpfer (The Peace Fighter) were illegally produced in Berlin and Düsseldorf and reported on Nazi atrocities in the occupied territories.

(Right) ''Where the German soldier stands, no one else gets in'' reads the poster behind the sentry in this propaganda photograph. Similar ones appeared of sentinels on the Atlantic Wall.

(Right) An Illustrierter Film-Kurier cover featuring Verräter (Traitor) directed by Karl Ritter and released on 9 September 1936. It starred Willy Birgel, described as "Germany's Clark Gable," and a future mistress of Goebbels, Czech actress Lida Baarova.

(Far right) The front cover of the Münchner Illustrierte Presse of 5 January 1943 features Zarah Leander in her last film (Damals) before returning to Sweden. Damals like Die Grosse Liebe was directed by Rolf Hansen, but it failed to equal its popularity.

(Right) An advertisement still from Boleslav Barlog's film Junge Herzen (Young Hearts), which was released on 30 November 1944. Described as "a remarkable little picture about a bitter-sweet love affair set in Berlin and its environs," it starred Harald Holberg, Ingrid Lutz and Lisca Malbran.

*19 July 1944: popular magazine* Die Woche's *cover featuring a fully-equipped naval officer.*

*The front cover of* Die Woche *of 26 July 1944 showing a girl harvester. Inside this issue was a pledge of loyalty to Hitler following the 20 July bomb plot.*

*(Opposite)* A young girl eating rations at a street soup kitchen.

*(Above)* Members of the Nazi-Frauenschaft *(the women's organisation),* the BDM *(League of German Maidens),* and the Luftwaffe *preparing and distributing food after an air raid. Note the camouflaged tents in the background.*

(Opposite) *Nazi high society: on 3 June 1944, Eva Braun's sister Gretl married SS General Hermann Fegelein, Himmler's representative at Führer Headquarters. The civil wedding took place at Salzburg town hall and a reception was given at the Berghof, where Hitler toasted the couple. Here the guests, including Himmler (center, left, with glasses) are seen at the dining table.*

*Later there was dancing to a small band of SS musicians.*

(Above) *The real party took place that night in the "Eagle's Nest." From left to right: actor Heini Handschuhmacher, Eva Braun, Fegelein, Gretl Braun.*

# 1944–1945

Berlin's famous "rubble women" form a chain to clear rubble from bomb-damaged buildings. Ninety-five per cent of the city's center had been destroyed, and in the rest of the capital only one house in four was habitable.

# "Enjoy the war while you can – the peace will be terrible"

In the spring of 1944 the devastation was so great and increasing so rapidly, not only in the capital but throughout the Reich, that the Propaganda Ministry commissioned fifty of Germany's best photographers to take pictures of works of art and buildings (mainly churches and castles) that were still standing and intact. In future these pictures might be the only evidence that such treasures had ever existed. At the same time the regime still tried to "exploit every human feeling for purposes of propaganda," with such displays as a sailor's choir singing on behalf of the *Winterhilfe* (Winter Aid) campaign in the lower subway of the Friedrichstrasse station.

The spring of 1944 was a long one, and exceptionally cold, and a Danish correspondent P. E. von Stemann recalled it as a time of

> dullness, anticipation, fear and continuous bombing. It was a soulless existence. The war seemed perpetual. The sameness of each successive day was blunting but the obliteration of all beauty was even more so. . . . The flowers had gone, the books had been burnt, the pictures had been removed, the trees had been broken, there were no birds singing, no dogs barking, no children shrieking . . . there were no small surprises, no fun, no merriment . . . there was no laughter and no giggling. No face ever lit up in a warming smile, no friendly kiss or hug. There was still the sky above . . . but then it was often effaced by the stinking and greasy carpets of voluminous black smoke.

For those who had it, money was spent without thinking twice. Ursula von Kardorff was asked by a compositor on the *Deutsche Allgemeine Zeitung* if she could give him the name of a good dressmaker. When told that she knew of one but that the dressmaker was very expensive, charging 200 marks for a dress, the compositor replied "That doesn't matter. What else is there to do with the money anyhow?" Ordinary soldiers, on leave from the Russian front, handed out tips equaling a fortnight's pay, and a waiter in a pub at the Gendarmenmarkt in Berlin was able to buy a small place in the country with the tips he received for producing bottles of Moselle wine. Von Stemann noticed how

> people would hold on to and safeguard whatever they owned and treasured. Some had cursed luck: a couple in Berlin had evacuated their four small children . . . aged between 1 and 11 years to their grandparents' farm in Silesia. A stray bomb fell on the farm and killed all four children, the grandparents and a 14-year-old cousin. The parents in Berlin survived unharmed.

Despite everything, however, cultural life still went on: the Berlin Philharmonic, wearing hats and overcoats, played Hadyn's *Seasons* in the Cathedral, Shakespeare's *Winter's Tale* was performed, with Wilfried Seyffert as Autolycus, and in the rebuilt State Opera, bombed out three years before, Herbert von Karajan gave a concert on 13 March. A month before, the conductor had complained to von Studnitz about the attitude of Wilhelm Furtwangler, the conductor of the Berlin Philharmonic, who was doing all he could to injure von Karajan's career, having closed the doors of the Philharmonic to him and refused him permission to conduct in Vienna. Furwangler's jealousy had been aroused by an article in a newspaper entitled "The miracle named Karajan!"

But below the surface, speculation and anticipation abounded and throughout the Reich the forthcoming Allied invasion of Europe was everywhere the topic of conversation and of private thoughts. Christabel Bielenberg, an Englishwoman married since 1934 to a German and anti-Nazi, found herself delivering diatribes to "some lonely tree or maybe a wayside crucifix" in walks near the village of Rohrbach in the Black Forest. These diatribes

> invariably petered out in a bout of prolonged snivelling. "Oh come on, please come, please hurry—I'm so sick of it all—this ruddy place's a madhouse—I just want to be back amongst my own people, my own people do you hear?" . . . The newspaper at any rate had a word for my disease, for there was no doubt that I was suffering from my own brand of what Dr Goebbels, in his wisdom, was describing as "invasionitis."

Not even "invasionitis" could, however, it seem, undermine the renowned German bureaucracy as exemplified in a printed memorandum from the Major of Schöneburg in late April 1944:

*Berlin, 20 April 1944, Hitler's 55th birthday. The banner, with unconscious irony, reads: "We greet the first worker of Germany—Adolf Hitler." Others bore the slogan: "Our walls may break, but never our hearts!"*

*(Right) Two elderly members of the* Volkssturm.

*(Below) A group of* Volkssturm, *Germany's Home Guard. Consisting mainly of poorly-equipped young boys and old men the* Volkssturm *was not a very effective fighting force.*

With reference to your communication of 19.4.1944, I regret that I am
unable to accede to your request for the issue of coupons for a new frying-
pan. The satisfaction of the requirements of the armed forces and the
devotion of the whole German industry to the needs of total warfare
demand, today more than ever, that the individual modify his way of life
and restrict his demands to the absolute minimum. I trust that you too, Sir,
will appreciate this and will refrain from submitting even justifiable
demands. No appeal against this decision can at present be considered.

At last, on 11 May, the ''barbaric cold'' finally abated and green shoots were seen
springing up among the ruins. A week later there was an invasion scare, but it
turned out to be a false alarm. von Studnitz noted that the prospect of an Allied
landing was still faced with confidence, and that everyone hoped that when the
invasion was repulsed on the Atlantikwall there would be a turn in the tide of the
war in Germany's favor. June 5 1944 saw the Propaganda Minister conferring with
Hitler at the latter's villa, the *Berghof* on the Obersalzberg. Goebbels returned at 2.30
in the morning to his guesthouse telling his press officer Dr Rudolf Semler that he
wanted to see press telegrams in his bed at nine o' clock, but as Dr Semler recalled in
his diary:

> After four o' clock there was no more sleep for us . . . at five minutes past
> four I suddenly received the first reports of Allied landing operations on
> the Channel coast. There is no doubt the invasion has begun. I at once ring
> Goebbels and tell him the sensational news . . . I can almost see him,
> through the telephone, jumping out of bed; then, after a few seconds the
> voice comes over: ''Thank God, at last. This is the final round.''

The press were instructed to write pieces ''greeting this long-awaited event with
positive pleasure.'' The tone adopted, according to von Studnitz, was ''Hurrah!
Here it comes at last. Now we'll show them, and throw them all back into the sea. At
last final victory approaches.''

Whilst the Reichspost stopped all private telephone calls to keep lines free, von
Stemann noticed in the capital: ''The reaction . . . was strange. The apathetic
Berliners showed that day some sporadic excitement and . . . it was claimed that the
war now would be won within weeks.'' Ten days later German newspaper offices
received confidential press releases: ''The apocalypse has begun,'' they read, ''We
are bombarding London with long range guns [sic] which will shortly destroy the
city.'' The long-awaited reprisals had begun. The Frankfurt SD reported a boost in
morale:

> It was moving to hear the simple workers expressing their joy that their
> unshakable faith in the Führer had now found renewed confirmation. One
> old worker remarked on the train on his way home from work: ''How often
> I've argued with my co-workers because they no longer believed in
> revenge, in our Führer, not even in German victory. When the terror
> attacks on Frankfurt were getting worse, I myself began to doubt, but my
> inner conviction kept telling me: What the Führer promises, he does. And
> now I am overjoyed that revenge has truly come, and I firmly believe that
> it will bring us victory.''

Others regretted that they could not ''get even with the Americans.''

But in Berlin, the reprisals were met with less enthusiasm; people feared that an Allied retaliation to the bombing of London would be directed at Berlin. Gas warfare became a particular concern. Sure enough, in retaliation for the V1 Flying Bomb (*Vergeltungswaffe Nr. 1*) raids on London, on 21 June Berlin received its heaviest daylight raid yet, lasting from 9 am to 11.15 am. The dark smoke was so thick on the Wilhelmstrasse that flashlights were necessary; Ursula von Kardorff described the scene:

> Blue-black columns of smoke were swirling up all around us, lit by gouts of brilliant flame—it was just like a mediaeval picture of hell-fire. Olive-green dust and whitish plaster-rubble cover the streets several feet deep, but there was a kind of savage beauty about the whole scene.

She sourly observed that both Hitler's Reich Chancellery and the Propaganda Ministry remained undamaged, commenting: ''The Devil himself must be protecting them.''

This feeling must have been confirmed a month later when at 12.42 pm on 20 July 1944 a bomb planted in a conference hut at the Führer's Headquarters at Rastenburg in East Prussia by Colonel Count Claus von Stauffenberg exploded killing four men instantly and seriously injuring others. The Führer, despite having a ''backside like a baboon'' as he put it, escaped with nothing more than a few cuts.

The attempt on Hitler's life came as a great shock to most Germans. News first reached the public later that afternoon. Von Studnitz heard a special announcement on the radio as he sat in the foyer of the Hotel Elefant in Weimar after attending a society wedding; von Kardorff heard the news at the offices of the *Deutsche Allgemeine Zeitung* before 5 pm; von Stemann was working at the Hotel Esplanade when a colleague telephoned from the Press Club just after 4 pm with the news. Among ordinary Berliners, however, there was apparently very little reaction, with no shouting, no crowds, and no excitement. ''One reason was that the Berliners did not know what was happening till it was all over . . . it must have been the most obscure attempt at a coup ever . . . It was the greatest-ever non-event, a non starter,'' commented von Stemann. Public reaction was summed up in an official report:

> All reports uniformly make reference to the sudden dismay, emotional shock, deep indignation, and anger unleashed among the whole population by the report of the assassination attempt. From several cities there are reports of women bursting into tears in stores and on the streets, some completely out of control. The joy at the mild outcome was extraordinarily great. Heaving a heavy sigh of relief, the people ascertained: ''Thank God, the Führer is alive.''

According to the same source, workers in the northern districts of Berlin now saw no sense in ending the war, short of a complete victory. Germany could not afford a civil war. The assassins must have been crazy for how could the war continue without the Führer? And indeed, many did believe that Hitler's death would mean certain defeat.

Fanatical Nazi, thirteen-year-old Heinz Kupper, disobeying the law and tuning in to London, was, moreover, not disappointed in the Allied reaction:

Also London did not make very much of that handful of officers, who in any case were already dead. They were given their due; one sub-man praises another, but even the praise sounded superior and condescending. Even the enemy thought them irrelevant and insignificant upstarts, base-minded men of straw who had made a futile attempt . . . The best thing would be to forget the whole thing as quickly as possible.

Meanwhile Dr Ley, who had already attacked the plotters as "dirty dogs of blue blood" in a drunken speech at a Berlin armaments factory on 21 July, now reappraised the morale situation following the plot in an article entitled "Now we know that the mass assault of Bolshevism can be stopped" in *Der Angriff* of 30 July:

Thus we are indeed excellently prepared for the imminent last round of this national struggle. And we can truly say this time that those mad men and criminals, whilst they were intent upon evil, effected good.

Shortly after the plot's failure, the conspirators came before the People's Court where Roland Freisler ranted, raved and berated them, before pronouncing the death sentence. On Hitler's express orders they were hung from meat hooks by piano wire, and were filmed in their death throes. The finished film was rushed to the Führer's Headquarters for Hitler's delectation.

In the capital the hero of the event was the city's Gauleiter, Goebbels, who now received the powers he had so much wanted after Stalingrad and was named Reich Trustee of Total War. It was, in his opinion, not a day too early:

If I had received these powers when I wanted them so badly, victory would be in our pockets today, and the war would probably be over. But it takes a bomb under his arse to make Hitler see reason.

*After the failure of the attempt on Hitler's life in July 1944, conspirator Field-Marshal Erwin von Witzleben appears before the People's Court (8 August). The accused were deprived of their ties, belts and braces to prevent suicide and further their indignity. Some 4980 people, including von Witzleben, were executed in the immediate aftermath of the bomb plot.*

The scene was now set for "the last, most total, total mobilization;" in the late summer and early autumn of 1944 Germany braced itself for the last decisive battle. In the *Berliner Börsen Zeitung* of 29 August an SS war correspondent wrote an article entitled "The secret of the final struggle" which finished with the words:

> ... At least we know why we must now make our last, great effort. To do so is not beyond our power. In this war never once have we given up at the critical moment. And whatever the last price may be, we are prepared to pay it, with every means and with all the strength at our disposal. *Victory now really is very near.*

Measures for "Total Mobilization" now came thick and fast: the age limit for the compulsory labor of women was raised from forty to fifty; all non-German domestic workers—servants, governesses etc—were to shift to war industries; more sections of manufacture for civilian consumption were to be suspended or combed again for armaments workers. And on 12 August further reductions in all public services including the post and railways were announced. The posting of small packages, printed matter, samples and catalogs was henceforth prohibited. Parcel post, and deliveries were cut down to one daily delivery only in the cities (with one day per week entirely omitted) and a weekly delivery in the country. All letter boxes were closed, to save the petrol used in emptying them by van, but as von Studnitz observed, this was a false economy: "That millions of people will now have to wear out their irreplaceable shoes walking to a post office to post their letters does not seem to have occurred to anybody in authority." The five thousand periodicals produced before the war were now reduced to 500, the majority of which were trade, technical and medical journals. Advanced subscriptions for suspended periodicals were not refunded, unless by a special request, and by February 1945, an amount of 1,355,704 marks, taken from subscriptions, had been handed by the publishers to the German Red Cross and *Winterhilfe*.

Nor did Goebbels neglect the arts in his drive for "Total Mobilization." Artists of all kinds—from painters and poets to musicians and actors—were to be drafted into munitions: the Charlottenburg Opera was closed, for example, and its members called up to work at the Berlin Siemens factory. A special decree proclaimed:

> The style of our public life must be fitted to the requirements of total war.
> All functions not directly serving our common war effort—such as
> receptions, public inductions of officials, music and theater festivals,
> exhibition opening and memorial celebrations—must cease.

Accordingly, all theaters, opera houses, music halls and other places of entertainment were closed on 1 September 1944. An estimated 30,000 workers were thus gained for the war industries but public morale continued to suffer.

To counter this drop in morale, Goebbels, ever keen to set a good example, staged another publicity stunt. After Stalingrad and the first "Total War" period, his wife Magda had gone off by tram to work at the Telefunken radio factory in Berlin but had called it off when none of the other leaders' wives followed her example. Now in August 1944 Goebbels wanted to set up a home workshop for shell fuzes in his house under Magda's direction, but this too came to nothing. Instead the cook was released to go into the armaments industry, but as Dr Semler recorded:

Two days later she came back with a beaming face and told her former colleagues that she had not gone into a factory, but had been given a job as a cook for Dr Best, [the Reich representative in Denmark]. Goebbels heard of this and was furious. He accused Best of sabotaging the Total War effort. I was told to inform Best on behalf of Goebbels that he must do without a new cook. So now she has a job in the canteen at the Siemens works serving out beer. But in official statistics she is counted as a munitions worker.

With all other places of entertainment closed the radio became "the sole purveyor of musical entertainment to the public," and a "discerning minority" looked forward all week to *Das Schatzkästchen* (Treasure Trove), a Sunday morning feature in which "good music was interspersed with suitable poetic and dramatic excerpts culled from the German classics." Retaining its popularity, *Wunschkonzert* was still heard on Sunday afternoons. The Wehrmacht communiqué with its tale of "strategic withdrawals to pre-prepared positions" finished the day's programme invariably and was ironically followed by a recording of Maria von Schmedes singing "Another beautiful day draws to its close."

The cinema still provided a haven for war-weary civilians, the most popular films being those that eschewed a war theme: *Wir Machen Musik* (We're Making Music) with Ilse Werner, and *Romanze in Moll* (Romance in Moll), based on a Maupassant story *Les Bijoux* (The Jewels), were both directed by Helmut Kautner. *Junge Adler* (Young Eagles) about the rehabilitation of the delinquent son of a rich aeroplane manufacturer through his work as a laborer in his father's factory starred

*Kristina Soderbaum and Carl Raddatz in a scene from Veit Harlan's* Immensee, *a color film. Harlan (Soderbaum's husband) was blacklisted after the war because of his part in directing Nazi propaganda films including the notorious* Jud Süss. *In 1950 he was tried for crimes against humanity but was acquitted by a Hamburg court due to lack of evidence.*

*(Opposite) Elderly civilians and Hitler Youths hurriedly conscripted to undertake the construction of defences behind the Western Front waiting for their train in September 1944.*

the perennially popular Willy Fritsch, and featured a very young Hardy Krüger. Fritsch had allegedly become a casualty of Total War, as Princess Marie ''Missie'' Vassiltchikov recorded in her diary. A friend had moved to

the actor Willy Fritsch's house in Grünewald, a charming little cottage he left in a hurry after having a nervous breakdown during one of the recent raids. Apparently, he lay sobbing on his bed all day until his wife came back to Berlin and took him out to the country.

The twenty-fifth anniversary of the film company Ufa had been celebrated on 5 March 1943 with the release of a color film *Munchhausen* starring the most popular of all male wartime stars, Hans Albers, in the title role with a star-studded cast including Brigitte Horney as Catherine the Great. Ironically, the scriptwriter of *Munchhausen* was Erich Kästner, author of *Emil and the Detectives*, who was on the official blacklist of writers. The director Josef von Baky nevertheless suggested to Goebbels that Kästner might be the ideal man to do a script and the Propaganda Minister agreed. Kästner himself however had picked the subject matter: ''Well, your commission has come from the world's greatest liar—why not do a film about his closest competitor, the Baron Munchhausen?'' Other color films included Veit Harlan's *Die goldene Stadt* (The golden Town), *Immensee* and *Opfergang* (Sacrifice) all of which starred Harlan's Swedish wife Kristina Soderbaum, who had become a star overnight in the pre-war film *Jugend* (Youth). Hans Ruchmann's comedies, especially *Der Gasmann* (The Gas Man) and *Quax, der Bruchpilot* (Quax, the crash pilot), remained popular with the public, and he with the regime; in March 1943 he was given a tax-free gift of forty thousand marks. Fellow actor Emil Jannings received sixty thousand.

Outside the cinema there was precious little to laugh at. The *Berliner Morgenpost* of 5 September announced ''that war within the confines of the Reich had become a citizens' war'' with the approach of the Allied armies in the west to the Siegfried Line and the Russians in the east converging on East Prussia and Poland. The raids continued and scenes in the shelters at Hanover's main station reminded a witness of Gorki's *Night Asylum*: ''Dozens fainted. At the shelter entrances complete panic.''

To combat the ''Anglo-Saxons'' in the west and the ''Bestial Bolsheviks'' in the east, the *Volkssturm* (Home Guard) was established on the anniversary of the Battle of Leipzig (18 October) under the leadership of Himmler, Martin Bormann and Wilhelm Schepmann, the SA Chief of Staff. It was supposed to consist of all men between the ages of 16 and 60—''the last round-up of the old and the lame, the children and the dotards.'' On 12 November Goebbels attended the swearing-in ceremony of the Battalion, Wilhelmplatz 1 of the *Volkssturm* under the command of his own State Secretary, Dr Werner Naumann. To the tune of ''Durch Gross-Berlin marschieren wir'' (We're marching through Greater Berlin), the *Volkssturmmänner* marched past the Minister who had described them as a ''thoroughly modern troop with the spirit of 1813 but the weapons of 1944.'' Ironically, they then had to turn in their weapons, which had only been lent for the occasion. With a sort of gallows humor that afternoon *Wunschkonzert* featured Wilhelm Strienz singing ''Erst einmal ganz sachte'' (Take it easy to start with). SD reports showed that people in Stuttgart questioned ''the sincerity and commitment of the propertied classes'' to the

*(Opposite) August 1944: Hitler Youths and elderly civilians digging tank traps in the Moselle Valley.*

*Volkssturm*, while the rural population ''regarded the whole thing as an admission of weakness.'' In Württemberg it was ridiculed as the latest *Wunderwaffe* (wonder weapon), and, from the dress regulations alone, it is not difficult to see why the new organization became the target of such mockery. The *Neue Wiener Tageblatt* for instance, advised its readers that:

> Uniformity of clothing in the *Volkssturm* is, in itself, of no importance: but camouflage is. To wear bright or very light-colored clothing is inadvisable. It has therefore been decided that light-colored clothing such as the Party uniform, shall be dyed the new standard *einsatzbraun* [field-service brown]. The dyeing of civilian suits, however, will only be carried out if the original color is unsuitable for field service and provided that the suit, after being dyed, can still be worn by its owner for his lawful, civilian occasions.

At the same time the press published new rules regarding the employment of domestic servants. With ''Total War'' mobilization measures being pushed through elsewhere, these rules seemed a little incongruous for they laid down such minutae as the precise amount of time a servant must sleep after ten hours work (8 hours sleep); an eighteen-year-old maid must not be disturbed at night by her employer; the authorized two free afternoons a week could be converted into a day off, and so on. At the same time Government officials with thirty years' service no longer had the right to specific periods of leave.

On 24 October Aachen, the old imperial capital and seat of Charlemagne, surrendered to the U.S. First Army—the first German city to fall into Allied hands. About a week earlier the Red Army had launched a massive offensive along a ninety-mile front on the eastern frontier of East Prussia, a province which until then had been relatively sheltered from the war. On the 19th the Russians broke into the Reich and captured the districts of Gumbinnen and Goldap.

A vigorous counter-attack by the German Fourth Army commanded by General Friedrich Hossbach, (who had previously proposed the precautionary evacuation of civilians from the eastern parts of East Prussia, only to be told that such proposals smacked of defeatism), pushed the Soviets out of German territory by 5 November 1944. The liberating troops came across the village of Nemmersdorf, one of the first villages in Germany to experience the severity of Soviet occupation. Its inhabitants—all women and children—had been slaughtered in the most gruesome bestial manner. Many had been crucified. Moreover, fifty French prisoners of war had also been murdered trying to protect them. The few survivors of the massacre had taken flight westwards.

The authorities immediately invited neutral correspondents and doctors from Switzerland, Sweden and Spain ''to witness the frightful scene,'' but the outside world, which was just receiving positive proof of the Nazi extermination camps in Poland—*The Illustrated London News* of 14 October had an illustrated report on Majdanek, near Lublin—took little notice of Nemmersdorf. In Germany and especially East Prussia the name ''came to evoke unspeakable fear;'' the mass flight of the civilian population of Germany's eastern provinces was a direct consequence.

Internally, propaganda decrying the ''monstrous Soviet lust for blood'' and the

*A poster from the mid-war period reads: ''Shame on you, bigmouth. The enemy is listening—silence is your duty.''*

''Bolshevik aim of destroying and exterminating the *Volk*'' was played up for all it was worth, but, nevertheless, fell far short of Nazi expectations. The Stuttgart SD report found that:

> Citizens are saying it is shameful to feature these so prominently in German newspapers.... What motive does the leadership have in publishing pictures like those in the *N.S. Kurier* on Saturday? They must surely realize that every intelligent person, upon seeing these victims, will immediately think of the atrocities that we have committed on enemy soil, yes, even in Germany. Did we not slaughter the Jews by the thousands? Don't soldiers repeatedly tell of Jews who had to dig their own graves in Poland? And what did we do with the Jews who were in the concentration camp in Alsace? After all, Jews are also human. We have only shown the enemy what they can do with us, should they win.

Germany was now entering the sixth winter of the war, and as von Studnitz noted: ''the ring is steadily closing around us ... the military situation is very serious.'' He noted too, on 12 December, that the meat ration was being distributed in ''suspiciously generous quantities,'' an informant telling him that this was due to the mass slaughter of ''refugee cattle'' driven in from the former occupied territories. And then suddenly on Saturday 16 December the German forces in the west under Field-Marshal Gerd von Rundstedt launched an offensive against the U.S. Forces on the Ardennes front. For a very brief spell the supposed success of the offensive came to the German people as ''rainfall after a long drought.'' While there was no public rejoicing as the situation was still too grave, morale was given a tremendous boost, ''a wonderful Christmas present,'' and there were even words of praise for the much maligned Luftwaffe. As an official SD report put it:

> Even a minor success would be welcomed with gratitude by the population. That we are actually in a position to undertake such a military operation has all at once significantly raised confidence in the leadership and in the strength of the Reich.''

Christmas was:

> generally observed in good spirits and full confidence in the future ... even if in areas endangered from the air the Christmas holidays were overshadowed by constant air-raid alarms and the depressing awareness of constant danger from the skies.... The German western offensive has made a profound impression even on the citizens who are outright pessimists and who believed the leadership remained silent because it has a great deal of unpleasantness to hide; in general, the diminished trust in the Wehrmacht, in the political leadership, and especially the N.S.D.A.P. has greatly increased ...

The Ardennes offensive had now failed; on 12 January 1945 after a five-hour artillery barrage, the Russians opened a massive offensive on the Eastern Front. German intelligence estimated that Russian superiority in infantry was eleven to one, in tanks seven to one, and in artillery twenty to one. The German front collapsed and with it the last shreds of hope for a ''stalemate victory;'' an observer noted:

Events in the east have robbed many people of their last shreds of composure. . . . Now . . . even the present generation, which has not hitherto given much thought to the war realizes that our agony has begun.

For some, the agony had been constant and, even at this late stage, the persecution of the Jews continued. On 19 January Andreas-Friedrich recorded in her diary:

On January 15th the Jewish spouses in privileged marriages were to be taken away to the Jew camp at Theresienstadt. The trucks were ready; gasoline was available. Gasoline is always available when Jewish matters are involved. Then supposedly the Foreign Office puts its oar in—under pressure from the Allies, people are whispering. The lives of ten German POWs for each Jewish life. At last even the other side seems to have seen the light. So it's been called off again.

On 26 January the Red Army liberated the death camp of Auschwitz.

French writer François Lacheval had arrived in Berlin at the time of the Russian offensive and was amazed by ''the indifference of the masses in the presence of catastrophe.''

They went about their business, did their shopping amidst mountains of ruins, made their way along pavements obstructed with bricks and mud, as if nothing had happened. In a building with a gaping facade you might find, on the fourth floor, . . . a flat where gas, telephone and electricity were intact . . . The shops were empty. The windows (small apertures cut in enormous wooden panels) certainly exhibited some articles, but in practice one could buy nothing, except with the help of an *Ausgebombtenschein* [ticket certifying one had been bombed out], or at the smart shops of the Unter den Linden in exchange for cigarettes.

The city had also now become the haven for refugees fleeing the Red Army. Andreas-Friedrich recorded on 22 January 1945:

The first refugee trains are arriving from Silesia. An open car of frozen children has arrived at the Silesian Station. They stood in the cold for ninety-six hours, packed like sardines in a can. The wind blew on them, the snow covered them up: they froze and wept, they stood on their feet and died, jammed into a wooden coal car. Who can tell meaning from senselessness any more?

Silesian newspapers advised their female readers to leave all areas east of the Oder in accordance with an evacuation order. All women and children were urged to leave on foot and head south or west—waiting for trains was pointless. Further attempts at evacuation took place by sea, using the 790 merchant and naval ships gathered together by Admiral Doenitz, commander-in-chief of the Kriegsmarine (Navy). Despite the best efforts of the Kriegsmarine, however, it was impossible to stop Russian submarines infiltrating the shipping lanes close to the Baltic Sea coast. In a number of attacks on German vessels, nearly 20,000 refugees, sailors and wounded soldiers drowned in the Baltic. The most costly loss was the sinking of the *Wilhelm Gustloff*. Displacing 25,484 tons she had been the pride of the pre-war *Kraft durch Freude* fleet. Heading west on 30 January 1945 with at least 5,001 passengers, (estimates vary as to the exact number—some put the figure as high as 8,000) she was sunk at six minutes past one that night by the Russian submarine *S13*, commanded by Captain Alexander Marinesko. All but 904 people on board perished in the icy waters. On 10 February the *General von Steuben* was sunk with 3,000 seriously wounded troops on board; only 300 survived. And on 16 April the *Goya* went down with 5,385 refugees and troops on board, of whom only 183 were saved. In all, about 2,500,000 civilians and troops were evacuated by sea in the operation.

Meanwhile, on the same night as the sinking of the *Wilhelm Gustloff*, there took place in Berlin the première of *Kolberg*, a color epic directed by Veit Harlan, which had as its theme the heroic resistance of the town of Kolberg to Napoleon in 1807. The film had been commissioned as far back as 1 June 1943 and Goebbels had noted in his diary: "I expect extraordinary things of this Harlan film. It fits exactly the political and military landscape we shall probably have to reckon with by the time the film can be shown." A copy of the film was flown in to the garrison of La Rochelle, still holding out, and Goebbels sent the garrison commander the following telegraph:

> My wish is that the film be accepted by you and your courageous soldiers as a document of the unwavering resolution of a people which, in these days of worldwide struggle, united with those fighting at the front, is willing to emulate the great example of its glorious history.

With Germany supposedly fighting a "Total War," Harlan's film cost 8·5 million marks; 187,000 soldiers were employed as extras; 6,000 horses were used, and 10,000 uniforms were made. For one scene Harlan asked for 4,000 sailors; Admiral Doenitz refused, but his refusal was overruled after an appeal to the Propaganda Ministry and the men were supplied. At a time when the railway system was in chaos and rations were short because it was impossible to ship foodstuffs to the cities, one hundred railway trucks of salt were sent to the set to provide the necessary "snow" for one scene. Even Harlan himself found it a little extraneous:

> Hitler as well as Goebbels must have been obsessed by the idea that a film like this could be more useful to them than even a victory in Russia. Maybe they too were now just waiting for a miracle because they no longer believed in victory in any rational way. In the cinema's dream-factory miracles happened at home more quickly than they did at the front.

But there was to be no miracle of salvation now. As early as 6 February furniture vans were moved into place on Berlin's Lutzowplatz to form road-blocks, and the next day the Foreign Office issued an internal memorandum on the curtailment of the capital's transport services. A week later, the city of Dresden, hitherto untouched because, as one rumor had it, an aunt of Churchill lived there, was attacked by the RAF and USAAF, the first bombs being dropped at 10.15 pm on 13 February. Altogether 650,000 incendiaries were dropped, creating a firestorm which guided the Allied planes for 300 kilometers. In addition 1,477·7 tons of high explosives rained down on the city, whose population had been swelled by thousands of refugees from the east and 26,000 Allied prisoners of war. The effect was devastating. Lacheval wrote that "at a conservative estimate the death toll was 120,000: the bodies were burnt on pyres erected in public squares." And Andreas-Friedrich noted:

*Tokens, sold in aid of the* Winterhilfe, *displaying (clockwise, from left): a Hitler Youth emblem; a Model 1935 steel helmet; an anti-tank gun; and the coat of arms of Tarnowitz in Lower Silesia.*

(Opposite) *The fanatical Nazi resistance movement ''Werewolves'' was completely futile, despite the lurid threats of Werner Naumann, Goebbels' State Secretary at the Propaganda Ministry who said in Munich on 23 March 1945: ''The enemy fully realizes that the occupation of Germany is an impossibility ... If the enemy should try, he will unleash a partisan war under the banner of the Werewolf, such as the world has never witnessed before.'' Here a captured ''Werewolf'' on the German-Czech border reveals a hidden cache of weapons to the Allied authorities.*

Last Tuesday they devastated Dresden most terribly. Three times in twenty-four hours they unloaded ton after ton of bombs, until there was hardy a whole house left in the city, and all the splendour of a centuries-old civilization had gone up in smoke, Thousands of people met their deaths; they ran like burning torches through the streets, stuck fast in the red-hot asphalt, flung themselves into the waters of the Elbe. They screamed for coolness; they screamed for mercy. Death is mercy. Death is good when you are burning like a torch. Dresden was a glorious city, and it's a little hard getting used to the idea that Dresden, too, no longer exists. I almost feel like crying.

Goebbels did cry. Semler recorded on 16 February:

For the first time I saw Goebbels lose control of himself when two days ago he was given the stark reports of the disaster in Dresden. The tears came to his eyes with grief and rage and shock. Twenty minutes later I saw him again. He was still crying and looked a broken man.

Goebbels wanted Germany to denounce the Geneva Convention, and take reprisals against Allied prisoners of war. Semler leaked the proposal to a Swedish correspondent, whereupon the news reached London and a sharp warning was issued. The plan was dropped.

The end could not now be long delayed, and yet futile attempts were still made to postpone its inevitable arrival. The ''Werewolves'' resistance organization was set up under SS Obergruppenführer Hans-Adolf Prutzmann with Goebbels' encouragement. Its purpose was to conduct guerrilla warfare behind the Allied lines, but its only outstanding success was the assassination of Dr Franz Oppenhoff, a lawyer who had been appointed Oberbürgermeister (chief mayor) of Aachen by the Americans.

*Breslau, despite being completely surrounded by the Red Army by 13 February 1945, held out under siege conditions until 7 May 1945. Here women and children in the city fetch supplies under the supervision of the Red Army.*

*The zonal division of Germany, 1945.*

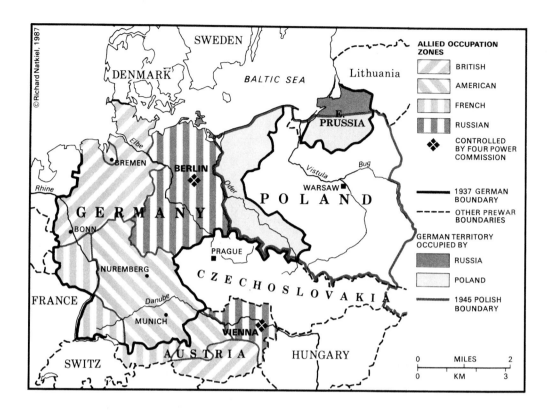

In most places, however, the arrival of the Anglo-American forces was greeted with relief by the German civil population. Even Goebbels' own birthplace Rheydt hung out white flags at the approach of the American troops, to his anger and disappointment:

> I am vexed most of all by the behaviour of the people in my home town of Rheydt. The Americans have struck up a real triumphal chorus about it. A certain Herr Vogelsang, known to me from the early days as a downright National-Socialist philistine, has placed himself at the disposal of the American occupation authorities as Oberbürgermeister. In doing so he stated that he had only joined the Party on compulsion from me and otherwise had nothing to do with it.

Nonetheless, there was a false aura of control. Even as late as February the State seemed to have the situation in hand. A coupon system was introduced for black market goods, butter, for example, and trains ran with remarkable punctuality, the non-stop Berlin–Hamburg pullman service was not being interrupted until March. In Berlin, the S Bahn continued to run all night. The Berlin Philharmonic still gave concerts at the Admiralspalast, and for less sophisticated musical tastes there were the Lecouna Cuban Rhythm Boys, employed to play at parties and weddings. One guest at such a wedding described how:

> around ten o'clock the siren broke up the festivities with its harsh warning. While the guests hesitated and time was wasted in deciding whether to take shelter, blast shook the house. As it was too late to leave, the orchestra played louder, all joined in the dancing and singing to drown out the sound of explosions, to drink and forget, until the deafeningly

sharp whistle of a fire-engine penetrated into the hot room. They looked out. The attack was over, but the house next door was hit, was on fire; the flames lit up the whole neighbourhood.

Lacheval, also present at these *fin de siecle* celebrations noted:

> The raids were terrifying, but the shelters were excellent, enormous cellars fitted with bunks, (the one under the Zoo had the cubic space of Selfridge's, and could accommodate 10,000 people).

The raids seemed continuous, and every German listened in to the hourly *Luftlage* (air situation) broadcast by all stations. As soon as a bomber formation penetrated the Reich, a special transmitter would give its exact situation, strength, altitude and direction. Germany was divided into alphabetically designated areas, with corresponding first names assigned to each area. Although the map was supposed to be secret, each household had charted a copy for itself, to enable the family to make advance preparations, or to pass the time playing the game of "Bertha, Bertha:"

> There was a red formation, a blue one, and a green one, red 2, blue 2, and so on, and bets were made as to the town over which they would make their swoop . . . At 'Gustav Friedrich' [the end of the game, "Gustav Friedrich" being the code name for Berlin] you packed up your bag, and joined in the national tide flowing to the shelters: Berlin would be sounding the alert in ten minutes.

One air raid fatality whose death "aroused considerable excitement" was People's Court president Roland Freisler. His death during the massive USAAF raid on Saturday 3 February was regarded by some "as an act of just retribution for the revolting manner in which he conducted the case against the July 20th accused."

As the barricades went up—which some alleged would save Berlin when the Russians died laughing at them—law and order and public utilities were breaking down. On 1 February all Berlin policemen on the beat began to wear steel helmets and carry carbines, and units of the Berlin *Volkssturm* were ordered to the front. Newspapers were reduced in numbers and appeared as single sheets, with abbreviated headlines and subtitles. DNB (*Deutsche Nachrichtenbüro*, the official German News Agency), supplied the entire press with war articles, and the rest of the papers merely contained the OKW communiqué hints to housewives and advertisements; even the radio programme was eliminated. The prestigious *Frankfurter Zeitung* had been closed down as early as 31 August 1943 on Goebbels' orders, and now in March 1945 the Berlin press consisted of five dailies and one weekly newspaper: the *Berliner Morgenpost*, the *Deutsche Allgemeine Zeitung* whose national edition had been suspended in February, and the Party's *Völkischer Beobachter* were the three morning papers. *12-Uhr Blatt* and *Berliner Illustrierte Nachtausgabe* (which had absorbed *Der Angriff* in February) were the afternoon ones. The weekly was the *Berliner Montagspost*. All carried the announcement:

> Any person who attempts to avoid fulfilling his obligations towards the community, and in particular any person who so acts from cowardice or for selfish reasons, must at once be punished with appropriate severity, in order to ensure that the State suffers no harm through the failure of the individual citizen.

Soon placards appeared on the hoardings of underground stations announcing that the twenty-five-year-old deserter Lieutenant Karl Ludwig had been shot while resisting arrest by a military patrol. The notice concluded with the warning that any soldier who left his country in the lurch in its hour of danger forfeited the right to live. On 17 March the SS combed Berlin, and arrested fifteen deserters in one block of houses alone.

A few days earlier the Propaganda Ministry had finally received a direct hit and for the first time the Wilhelmstrasse was closed to facilitate the work of the fire brigade and demolition squads. Frau Goebbels ''in her mink coat and green velvet hat . . . as though she were going to a cocktail party,'' inspected the damage. In the meantime her husband was having the walls of the city painted with slogans such as ''Capitulation? No.'' ''Victory or Siberia.'' But it was all to no avail as one by one German cities, towns, and villages, fell to the Allied armies. The death of President Roosevelt on 12 April 1945 raised Nazi hopes that a miracle might occur such as that which had saved Frederick the Great during the Seven Years' War when Tsarina

*1945 gave a new word to the dictionary: ''de-nazification.'' Here suspected Nazis fill in a questionnaire about their former political activities at a detention centre in May 1945.*

Elizabeth died. It was not to be. The next day the Russians captured Vienna, and three days later on Monday 16 April 1945 the last offensive began, its objective Berlin. The Red Army was only 38 miles from the capital when red flares were fired at 4 am signalling a "stupefying artillery barrage." The Berlin Philharmonic gave its last concert two days later, appropriately playing Wagner's *Die Götterdämmerung* (The Twilight of the Gods). All public utilities closed down, and the *Völkischer Beobachter* appeared for the last time on 26 April. Four days earlier the capital's 100-year-old telegraph office had closed down for the first time in its history. The last message to get through came from Tokyo and read "Good luck to you all." The same day the last civil airliner left Tempelhof Airport for Stockholm with nineteen passengers on board. The city's 1,400 fire brigades were ordered to the west. Unaffected by the battle chaos, operating without interruption, were the meteorological station situated at Potsdam, which did not miss a day's recording, and eleven of the capital's seventeen breweries, which continued producing beer—"an essential production," by government decree.

On 20 April the Führer celebrated his fifty-sixth and last birthday with all the Nazi chieftains present to deliver their congratulations. Ten days later, on 30 April 1945, with the Russians barely a block away from the bunker, Hitler, having married Eva Braun, took his life at approximately 3.30 pm. His wife also committed suicide. The next day, after poisoning their six children, Goebbels and his wife took their own lives. At 12.50 pm on 2 May General Weidling, Commandant of Berlin sent his chief of staff Colonel von Dufving to surrender to the Russians. Later that day loudspeakers announced the end of the fighting; the Red Flag was flying victoriously over the wrecked Reichstag building. Six days later on 8 May the fighting came to an end. The Third Reich had outlived its creator by barely one week. The "Thousand Year Reich" had lasted twelve years, four months and eight days. Germany was now entering the *Jahr Null* (Year Zero).

For millions of Germans now came the task of rehabilitation and reconstruction. The burden of the last twelve years of Nazi rule had to be shed. The country was divided into four zones, occupied by Britain, France, USA, and the Soviet Union, and over the next twenty years some 20,000 people would be convicted by either Allied or German courts for crimes committed during the Third Reich. In 1945 in the American zone 12 million *Fragebogen*—questionnaires containing 131 questions about the person's past life—were issued to all Germans over 18 years of age. A number of people had already flown the country or taken their own lives. Later that year the major war criminals, tried at Nuremberg, were sentenced by the International Military Tribunal. Goering evaded death on the gallows by committing suicide, but von Ribbentrop, Keitel, Jodl, Streicher and the others duly went to their deaths on 16 October 1946. A month earlier U.S. Secretary of State James F. Byrnes made a speech in Stuttgart in which he said:

> The American people want to help the German people to win their way back to an honorable place among the free and peace-loving nations of the world.

To the millions of Germans listening to a simultaneous translation "here at last was the outstretched hand they had been waiting for."

(Right) Life amidst the ruins: a Hamburg couple hang their laundry to dry in a flat without walls. The city's already desperate housing shortage was made worse by the large number of refugees from Eastern Germany and East Prussia who had been evacuated by the Kriegsmarine (Navy).

(Opposite) A Wehrmacht corporal sits in front of the ruined Reichstag building.

(Below) Autumn 1944. German civilians, including young boys, undertake salvage work following a hit by a misdirected German flying bomb. A similar incident had happened to Hitler himself on 17 June 1944 at Margival in France. A V1 on its way to London had turned around and landed on top of the Führer's bombproof underground bunker. No one was killed or wounded, but Hitler was so disturbed by the incident that he immediately left for his home on the Obersalzberg.

(Opposite) Osnabrück fell to the Allies on 4 April 1945. Many citizens took advantage of the chaos to stock up on supplies—here an elderly woman joins in the looting of a local brewery.

(Right) A motorist salvaging metal and spare parts from a wrecked car, damaged in the fighting.

(Below) From 5 March 1945 ration cards were no longer honored in many places in Germany and civilians were forced to go scavenging. Here two men are taking the meat from the carcass of a dead horse at the roadside.

(Above) German families expelled from Czechoslovakia walk alongside their wagons as the trek into Germany begins. The Nazi slogan "Back to the Reich!" takes on a new and ironic meaning.

(Opposite) Germany's rapidly declining military situation in the spring of 1945 brought with it a breakdown in law and order. Here German civilians loot a train carrying food supplies.

(Right) Berlin youngsters taking a drink at an emergency rehabilitation center. Germany's favorite pre-war non-alcoholic drink was Apfelsaft, a sweet apple juice, but supplies of this became short in 1941 and rhubarb juice was substituted.

*Red Army troops in Berlin in the last stages of the war. Der Panzerbär the last paper for the "defenders of Greater Berlin" claimed on 27 April 1945 that the capital would become a "mass grave for Soviet tanks."*

(Opposite) Red Army troops enter Berlin in late April 1945 as fires rage unchecked in the heart of the city. "I call on you to fight for your city. Fight with everything you have got, for the sake of your wives and your children, your mothers and parents . . . The battle for Berlin must become the signal for the whole nation to rise up in battle . . ." Goebbels, 23 April 1945.

(Right) On 26 April 1945, Germany's second largest port, Bremen, fell to Allied troops. Here, British soldiers take cover in the gas works in the final stages of combat.

On 28 March 1945 Eisenhower made the decision to strike out for Leipzig rather than Berlin. The city was taken on 19 April. When U.S. troops captured the city hall they found that the Oberbürgermeister (City Mayor), his wife, and sister-in-law had committed suicide in his office by taking poison.

(Opposite)  German civilians reading leaflets dropped by the Royal Air Force on VE Day (8 May 1945) announcing the end of hostilities.

(Above)  German civilians at Lüneburg listening to the broadcast news of Germany's surrender, 8 May 1945. Signing the surrender at Reims the previous day, Jodl had said to the Allied representatives: "At this hour, we can only hope that the victors will be generous."

(Right)  German citizens discussing the news of the surrender.

*(Right)  26 April 1945: teenage soldiers of the Wehrmacht and Luftwaffe surrender to the Allies. On 28 February 1945, 6000 sixteen-year-old boys had been called to the colors.*

*(Opposite)  "A twelve-year-old German boy approached a Canadian soldier and begged him for chocolate . . . the foolish Canadian began to rummage in his pockets. At this moment, the boy drew a pistol and shot the Canadian in the stomach. That, they claimed, was all you can expect of Germany's youth. Demoralized and wild. All I can say is: give us hundreds of thousands of lads like him, and we shall win the war!"*
    *Werner Naumann, 23 March 1945.*

*Here, a young boy-soldier surrenders to the Allies.*

*(Below)  A Luftwaffe major and eight boy auxiliaries are rounded up out of the woods by the British, 28 April 1945.*

*(Opposite) Two Red Army soldiers examine one of the large bronze eagles from the ruined Reich Chancellery. At its feet is a wreathed swastika.*

*(Right, and above) Allied troops assisting civilians with rescue work, 7 April 1945.*

*(Right)  A freed foreign laborer enjoying his first cigarette for months.*

*(Below)  Three Polish slave laborers on their liberation by British forces on 12 April 1945. In 1940 Himmler stipulated that Polish workers in the Reich should wear a distinctive badge, a violet "P" on a yellow diamond. Failure to wear this badge (worn here by two of the girls) carried a stiff fine of 150 marks or six weeks in jail.*

*(Opposite)  A Red Army soldier sweeps the Reich Chancellery steps clear of hundreds of boxes containing Nazi medal insignia in May 1945. Hitler's last investiture had taken place on 20 March when he decorated a number of Hitler Youths in the Reich Chancellery gardens. Werner Naumann, Goebbels' State Secretary, found the ceremony "one of the most moving situations I ever witnessed. The youngest, a 12-year-old Hitler cub ... had arrested a spy, and when Hitler asked him how he had discovered the man he replied 'He wore his corporal's stripes on the wrong arm, my Führer.'"*

*(Right) A woman clearing up her house after Allied possession.*

*(Below) U.S. troops examine Manet's* Wintergarden, *found with many other works in a salt mine in Bavaria. The Nazi leaders from Hitler and Goering downwards had indulged in large-scale looting of art. The Führer had intended his prizes to go into a massive new art gallery at Linz.*

*A street in Bremen at the end of the war.*

*A street scene in Flensburg, where Hitler's successor, Doenitz, had his headquarters. The Grand Admiral and his "government" were arrested on 23 May 1945. Shops such as this, where goods could be exchanged for other articles rather than German marks, never failed to arouse interest.*

(Right) Female guards at Belsen concentration camp including the notorious Irma Grese (center), mistress of the commandant SS Hauptsturmführer Josef Kramer, "The Beast of Belsen." When units of the 11th British Armoured Division liberated the camp they found 40,000 starving prisoners and 10,000 unburied dead; 13,000 prisoners died in the weeks following the camp's liberation.

(Opposite) "Work brings freedom" reads the slogan on the gates of Dachau concentration camp. Before the camp's liberation on 29 April 1945 an International Committee of Dachau Prisoners had been secretly organized to prevent the last minute mass extermination of the prisoners planned by the SS.

(Right) For many of Germany's foreign slave laborers liberation by the Allied armies meant a chance to get even with their former oppressors. Here Russian workers exact revenge on their Nazi overseer.

Buchenwald concentration camp, liberated on 14 April 1945 by the U.S. Army.

"Externally, Barrack 61 is like the other barracks, roughly a hundred-and-fifty feet long by thirty feet wide. Inside, four tiers of wooden shelves incline slightly toward the central corridor. In the rush season this single barrack housed twenty-three hundred 'non-workers' that tuberculosis, dysentery, pneumonia and plain starvation had rendered incapable of the daily twelve-hour stretch at the armament factory or nearby quarries. . . ."
Colonel Charles Codman, U.S. Army.

*Boy prisoners at Dachau greet the liberating U.S. troops. Although not an extermination camp like Auschwitz or Treblinka, thousands died at Dachau including those who had been forced to take part in the pseudo-scientific experiments carried out by SS doctors.*

*The bureaucracy of extermination: a double page from the death record book of a concentration camp. Most of the victims here are Russian, and the causes of death are, more often than not, paraphrased ''tuberculosis'' or ''pneumonia.''*

*(Above)  Prayers are held by a German priest over the graves of 800 slave laborers massacred at Passau on the German-Austrian border. Troops of the U.S. 3rd Army ordered local people to dig individual graves so that each of the murdered men might have a decent burial.*

*(Right)  Allied troops supervise food distribution in newly-liberated Belsen concentration camp. So acute had been the food situation that, according to H. O.de Druillenec, an inmate from Jersey, Channel Islands, at the trial of the guards, instances of cannibalism had taken place.*

One of the first acts of the Allied Control Commission in Germany was to distribute to cinemas a special newsreel compilation Die Todesmühle *(The mill of death)*. Film historians Roger Manvell and Heinrich Fränkel noted: "Public reaction to the newsreel naturally varied. Many saw the film in silence without visible emotion. Some women wept; others laughed hysterically, then burst into tears. Men were seen sitting with bowed heads, covering their faces with their hands." Here the citizens of Burgsteinfurt are forced to attend the showing of the film on 30 May 1945. Two girls who laughed when they came out of the cinema were compelled to see the film again.

(Opposite) "Swords into ploughshares" or in this case steel helmets into saucepans. Collected from the streets of Berlin in August 1945 the helmets, both Wehrmacht (Army) and Luftschutz (Civil Defence), are converted to domestic use.

(Right) An encampment of German prisoners near Lüneburg in May 1945. The prisoners await processing by the Allied military authorities. Himmler, disguised as a German policeman, was caught here; he managed to commit suicide on 23 May 1945 by biting on a vial of potassium cyanide poison.

(Right) In 1945 the Allies were faced with the formidable task of screening millions of Germans and tracking down Nazi war criminals. Here a British Field Security Intelligence sergeant interrogates Clara Lackman, a former typist in the Gestapo Headquarters at Lübeck.

*(Right)  A woman returns from the shops in the early days of occupation and surveys the rations she has managed to collect.*

*(Opposite)  German prisoners of war returning from England. 400,000 prisoners were held in Britain; many were employed on the land or helped to clear up Britain's bomb-damaged cities. After the war, 27,000 chose to remain in Britain rather than return to Germany.*

*(Right)  Rations for a family of four in the early days of occupation.*

# Statistics

**Nazi Germany at war, 1939–45: some facts and figures:** In September 1939 the population of "Greater Germany," including Austria, the Sudetenland and Memel, stood at 79,530,000, (that of Germany proper was 69,314,000). Germany was divided into 43 *Gaue*, which in turn were divided up into 890 *Kreise*. Within those *Kreise* were 30,601 *Ortsgruppen* (local groups), 121,406 *Zellen* (cells) and 539,774 Blocks, the smallest unit of the NSDAP and consisting of 30–40 households. At the outbreak of war there were approximately 3,900,000 Nazi Party members, who paid membership dues amounting to 23,616,000 Reichsmarks.

### Religion
Excluding Memel, a religious census taken just before the outbreak of war had Germany divided into the following denominations: Roman Catholic 31,944,000, Evangelical 42,636,000, Jewish 308,000, Without belief 1,208,000, Neo-pagans 2,746,000.

### Bomb damage
During the Second World War the following tonnage of bombs was dropped on Germany:

| | | | |
|---|---|---|---|
| 1940 | 10,000 tons | 1943 | 120,000 tons |
| 1941 | 30,000 tons | 1944 | 650,000 tons |
| 1942 | 40,000 tons | 1945 | 500,000 tons |

The following cities, excluding Dresden, the Rhineland and the Ruhr, suffered the highest air raid fatalities:

| | | | |
|---|---|---|---|
| Hamburg | 55,000 | Darmstadt | 12,300 |
| Berlin | 49,000 | Heilbronn | 7,500 |
| Magdeburg | 15,000 | Würzburg | 4,200 |
| Kassel | 13,000 | | |

Towns and cities with the highest numbers of air raid fatalities in the heavily bombed Rhineland and Ruhr were:

| | | | |
|---|---|---|---|
| Cologne | 20,000 | Gladbeck | 3,095 |
| Essen | 7,500 | Gelsenkirchen | 3,092 |
| Wuppertal | 7,000 | Aachen | 2,347 |
| Dortmund | 6,000 | Oberhausen | 2,300 |
| Dusseldorf | 5,863 | Krefeld | 2,084 |
| Bochum | 4,095 | | |

During the entire war 131 German cities and towns were subjected to major raids, including Berlin (29), Brunswick (21), Ludwigshafen (21), Mannheim (19), Cologne (18), Hamburg (16), Munich (16), and Hanover (11).

According to a general summary issued by the German Federal Republic's Statistical Office in *Wirtschaft und Statistik*, Volume 10, 1956, the highest total number of civilian dead and wounded in what was the Reich's territory on 31.12.1939 was:

| | |
|---|---|
| Dead | 537,000 |
| Wounded | 834,000 |

and on 31.12.42 was:

| | |
|---|---|
| Dead | 570,000 |
| Wounded | 885,000 |

A further report issued in 1962 gave the total number of civilian fatalities due to the air war as 539,000. In addition, it is estimated that 170,000 German Jews and 40,000 Austrian Jews died in the death camps or as a result of the "Final Solution." One estimate puts total German civilian losses 1939–45 at 3,640,000, and those of the Armed Forces at 3,050,000.

### Miscellaneous statistics

1. In November 1940 there were some 15.9 million radio licence holders in Germany. The fees (24 Reichsmarks, approximately £2 or $8) were collected by postmen.

2. In 1939 there were some 492 theaters and opera houses in "Greater Germany."

3. The *Winterhilfe* Campaign in Berlin for 1940–41 netted the following donations (in million Reichsmarks):

| | |
|---|---|
| Firms and organizations' donations | 15.78 |
| Donations from wages | 18.56 |
| "Sundays of Sacrifices" (*Eintopf*) | 12.22 |
| Reich street collections | 7.48 |
| Gau street collections | 1.02 |
| *Winterhilfe* stamps | 0.07 |
| Special efforts including "Police Day" and "Wehrmacht Day" | 4.00 |
| Total | 59.13 |

4. In 1943 Germany still produced 120,000 typewriters, 13,000 duplicating machines, 50,000 address machines, 30,000 calculating and accounting machines, 200,000 radios, 150,000 electrical bedwarmers, 3,600 refrigerators, 300,000 electricity meters, 12,000 tons of wallpaper and 4,800 tons of hair tonic. The total production of scissors — 4,400,000 — went to the Wehrmacht.

5. During the war, Germany employed the following numbers (in thousands) of foreign workers:

| Date | Total | Foreign civilians (including Jews) | Prisoners of war |
|---|---|---|---|
| 31.5.39 | 300 | 300 | — |
| 31.5.40 | 1,150 | 800 | 350 |
| 31.5.41 | 3,020 | 1,750 | 1,270 |
| 31.5.42 | 4,120 | 2,640 | 1,470 |
| 31.5.43 | 6,260 | 4,640 | 1,620 |
| 31.5.44 | 7,130 | 5,300 | 1,830 |

6. In November 1944 the allocation of German manpower in the war economy was as follows (numbers of workers):

| | |
|---|---|
| Army production | 1,940,000 |
| Air force production | 2,330,000 |
| Navy production | 530,000 |
| Shipbuilding | 250,000 |
| Mining industries | 970,000 |
| Iron industries | 470,000 |
| Trade, banks, insurance, catering | 3,180,000 |
| Domestic work | 1,450,000 |

7. An indication of the scale of compensation awarded to bombed-out civilians is given in the following figures (in Reichsmarks) issued by the Reich Administrative Court in October 1943:

| | |
|---|---|
| kitchen of medium quality | 450 |
| bedroom | 1,700 |
| night nursery | 470 |
| crockery, cutlery, cooking utensils | 400 |
| bed, table and personal linen | 1,900 |
| clothes | 1,000 |
| valuables | 500 |
| miscellaneous | 580 |
| Total | 7,000 |

(based on the average value of a household of three persons)

8. German newspaper circulation, 1939–40 (In 1939 2,400 papers issued 23,600,000 copies; in March 1943 1,400 papers had a total issue of 28,200,000.)

| | | |
|---|---|---|
| *Volkischer Beobachter* | 730,000 | NSDAP papers |
| *Rote Erde* | 243,000 | |
| *Westdeutscher Beobachter* | 237,000 | |
| *Essener Nationalizeitung* | 163,000 | |
| *Der Angriff* | 125,000 | |
| *Der Stürmer* (weekly) | 500,000 | |
| *Bremer Nachrichten* | 57,000 | |
| *Berliner Morgenpost* | 443,000 | |
| *BZ am Mittag* | 313,000 | |
| *Nachtausgabe* | 359,000 | |
| *Berliner Lokalanzeiger* | 208,000 | |
| *Deutsche Allgemeine Zeitung* | 100,000 | |
| *Frankfurter Zeitung* | 68,000 | |
| *Münchener Neueste Nachrichten* | 135,000 | |
| *Kölnische Zeitung* | 60,000 | |
| *Leipziger Neueste Nachrichten* | 146,000 | |

9. Just prior to the outbreak of the war the *Kraft durch Freude* (Strength through Joy) movement organized the following events:

| Form of entertainment | Performances | Attendance |
|---|---|---|
| concerts | 5,291 | 2,515,598 |
| folklore plays, songs, dances | 54,813 | 13,666,015 |
| opera and operetta | 12,407 | 6,639,067 |
| plays | 19,523 | 7,478,633 |
| variety shows | 18,910 | 7,980,973 |
| films | 3,586 | 857,402 |
| exhibitions | 555 | 1,595,516 |
| conducted tours | 676 | 58,472 |
| others | 15,084 | 11,118,636 |
| all forms of entertainment for 600 workers' camps | 13,589 | 2,658,155 |

In addition 1,029,583 performances of all kinds were given for 1,302,953 members of the Wehrmacht and *Reichsarbeitsdienst*.

# Bibliography

Adlon, Hedda, *Hotel Adlon*, London: Barrie Books, 1958.

Andreas-Friedrich, Ruth, *Berlin Underground*, New York: Henry Holt, 1947.

Bayles, William D., *Postmarked Berlin*, London: Jarrolds, 1942.

Bielenberg, Christabel, *The Past is Myself*, London: Chatto and Windus, 1968.

Bleuel, Hans Peter, *Strength through Joy*, London: Secker & Warburg, 1973.

Collins, Sarah Mabel, *The Alien Years*, London: Hodder & Stoughton, 1949.

Deuel, Wallace, *People under Hitler*, London: Lindsay Drummond, 1942.

Dollinger, Hans, *The decline and fall of Nazi Germany and Imperial Japan*, London: Odhams, 1968.

Flannery, Harry W., *Assignment to Berlin*, London: Michael Joseph, 1942.

Fredborg, Arvid, *Behind the Steel Wall*, London: Harrap, 1944.

Gersdorff, Ursula von, *Frauen im Kriegsdienst*, Stuttgart: Deutsche Verlags-Anstalt, 1969.

Grun, Max von der, *Howl like the wolves: growing up in Nazi Germany*, New York: William Morrow, 1980.

Grunberger, Richard, *The 12 Year Reich: a social history of Nazi Germany*, New York: Holt, Rinehart & Winston, 1971.

Grunfeld, Frederick V., *The Hitler file: a social history of Germany and the Nazis 1918–1945*, New York: Random House, 1974.

Gun, Nerin E., *Eva Braun: Hitler's Mistress*, London: Leslie Frewin, 1968.

Harsch, Joseph C., *Pattern of Conquest*, London: Heinemann, 1942.

Hassell, Ulrich Von, *The Von Hassell Diaries, 1938–1945*, London: Hamish Hamilton, 1948.

Herzstein, Robert Edwin, *The War that Hitler won*, New York: G. P. Putnam's Sons, 1978.

Heiber, Helmut, *Goebbels*, London: Hale, 1972. London: Hamish Hamilton, 1948.

Hoffmann, Heinrich, *Hitler was my Friend*, London: Burke, 1955.

Homze, Edward L., *Foreign Labor in Nazi Germany*, Princeton, NJ: Princeton University Press, 1967.

Horstmann, Lali, *Nothing for Tears*, London: Weidenfeld & Nicholson, 1953.

Hull, David Stewart, *Film in the Third Reich*, New York: Simon & Schuster, 1969.

Irving, David, *The Destruction of Dresden*, London: William Kimber, 1963.

Kardorff, Ursula von, *Diary of a Nightmare: Berlin 1942–1945*, London: Rupert Hart-Davis, 1965.

Koch, H. W., *The Hitler Youth: origins and development 1922–1945*, London: Macdonald & Jane's, 1975.

Koehn, Ilse, *Mischling, Second Degree*, London: Hamish Hamilton, 1977.

Laird, Stephen & Graebner, Walter, *Hitler's Reich and Churchill's Britain*, London: Batsford, 1942.

Leiser, Erwin, *Nazi Cinema*, London: Secker and Warburg, 1974.

Lochner, Louis (editor), *The Goebbels Diaries*, London: Hamish Hamilton, 1948.

McKee, Ilse, *Tomorrow the World*, London: Dent, 1960.

MacKinnon, Marianne, *The Naked Years*, London: Chatto & Windus, 1987.

Mandell, Richard D., *The Nazi Olympics*, London: Souvenir Press, 1972.

Manvell, Roger & Fraenkel, Heinrich, *The German Cinema*, London: Dent, 1971.

Maschmann, Melita, *Account Rendered*, London: Abelard Schuman, 1964.

Ministry of Economic Warfare, *Germany: basic handbook*, London: M.E.W., 1945.

Mosse, George L., *Nazi Culture*, New York: Grosset & Dunlap, 1966.

Oechsner, Frederick, *This is the Enemy*, London: Heinemann, 1943.

Padover, Saul K., *Experiment in Germany*, New York: Duell, Sloan & Pearce, 1946.

Peukert, Detlev J. K., *Inside Nazi Germany*, London: Batsford, 1987.

Pihl, Gunnar, *Germany: the last phase*, New York: Knopf, 1944.

Pope, Ernest R., *Munich playground*, London: W. H. Allen, 1942.

Raleigh, John McCutcheon, *Behind the Nazi Front*, London: Harrap, 1941.

Rumpf, Hans, *The bombing of Germany*, London: White Lion, 1963.

Rupp, Leila J., *Mobilizing Women for War: German and American Propaganda, 1939–1945*, Princeton, NJ: Princeton University Press, 1978.

Russell, William, *Berlin Embassy*, London: Michael Joseph, 1942.

Schutz, W. W. & B. de Seven, *German Home Front*, London: Gollancz, 1943.

Semmler, Rudolf, *Goebbels: the man next to Hitler*, London: Westhouse, 1947.

Senger, Valentin, *No. 12 Kaiserhofstrasse*, New York: Dutton, 1980.

Seydewitz, Max, *Civil Life in Wartime Germany: the story of the home front*, New York: The Viking Press, 1945.

Shirer, William L., *Berlin Diary*, New York: Knopf, 1941.

Smith, Howard K., *Last train from Berlin*, London: Cresset Press, 1942.

Sorge, Martin K., *The other price of Hitler's War*, New York: Greenwood Press, 1986.

Speer, Albert, *Inside the Third Reich*, New York: Macmillan, 1970.

Steinert, Marlis G., *Hitler's War and the Germans*, Athens, Ohio: Ohio University Press, 1977.

Stoddard, Lothrop, *Into the Darkness*, London: Chapman & Hall, 1941.

Studnitz, Hans Georg von, *While Berlin Burns*, London: Weidenfeld & Nicholson, 1963.

Taylor, Fred (editor), *The Goebbels Diaries 1939–1941*, London: Hamish Hamilton, 1982.

Taylor, Henry J., *Time runs out*, London: Collins, 1942.

Trevor-Roper, Hugh, *The Goebbels Diaries: the last days*, London: Secker & Warburg, 1978.

Vassiltchikov, Marie, *The Berlin diaries 1940–1945*, London: Chatto & Windus, 1985.

Whiting, Charles, *Hitler's Werewolves*, New York: Stein & Day, 1972.

Wolff-Monckeberg, Mathilde, *On the other side*, New York: Mayflower Books, 1979.

Zwerin, Mike, *La Tristesse de Saint Louis: Swing under the Nazis*, London: Quartet Books, 1985.

# Chronology

## 1939
**SEP**  1: Germany invades Poland.
3: Britain and France declare war on Germany.
**NOV** 30: Russia invades Finland.

## 1940
**APR**  9: Germany invades Norway and Denmark.
**MAY** 10: German invasion of Holland, Belgium and Luxembourg.
14: Holland capitulates.
27: British evacuation from Dunkirk.
28: Belgium capitulates.
**JUN** 10: Mussolini declares war on Britain and France. Auschwitz concentration camp opened in Poland.
21: Armistice terms presented to the French at Compiègne.
**AUG** 13: Major air assault begins on Britain.
24: First RAF bombing of Berlin.
**SEP**  7: Night *Blitz* begins on Britain.
15: Battle of Britain Day.
27: Germany, Italy and Japan sign a ten year military, political and economic alliance in Berlin.
28: Mussolini invades Greece.
15: Luftwaffe bomb Coventry.

## 1941
**MAR**  1: Bulgaria joins the Axis Pact.
9: US Senate passes the Lend-Lease Bill.
**APR**  6: Germany invades Yugoslavia and Greece.
17: Yugoslavia surrenders.
**MAY** 10: Rudolf Hess flies to Scotland and is held as a prisoner of war in Britain.
**JUN**  4: Kaiser Wilhelm II dies, aged 82, in Holland.
15: Croatia joins the Axis. Freezing of all German assets in the USA.
22: Germany invades Russia.
**JUL** 31: Heydrich ordered to prepare for the "final solution for the Jewish question."
**AUG** 14: Churchill and Roosevelt frame the "Atlantic Charter."
**SEP**  1: All Jews over six forced to wear a yellow star.
**OCT** 19: State of siege proclaimed in Moscow.
**DEC**  5: Germany and Italy agree to join Japan in any potential war with the USA.
6: Russian counter-offensive begins on the Moscow front.
7: Japanese attack Pearl Harbor.
11: Hitler declares war on the USA.
19: Hitler takes over personal command of the Army.

## 1942
**JAN** 20: Conference at Wannsee on the "Final Solution."
**FEB** 14: Fall of Singapore.
23: Heavy RAF raid on Rostock.
**MAY** 30/31: "1000 Bomber" raid on Cologne.
**JUN** 19: All prominent German Jews deported to "the East."
21: Rommel captures Tobruk.
**AUG** 22: Brazil declares war on Germany.
30: Russians bomb Berlin.
**OCT** 23: The Battle of El Alamein begins.
**NOV**  8: Allies land in French North Africa.
11: Germans occupy all of France.

## 1943
**JAN** 14–24: Allies call for the unconditional surrender.
18: Soviet troops raise the siege of Leningrad.
31: Paulus surrenders at Stalingrad.
**APR** 19: Uprising begins in the Warsaw Ghetto.
**MAY** 13: Axis forces in Tunisia surrender.
16: RAF attack on the Mohne and Eder dams.
**JUL**  5: Last major German offensive launched at Kursk.
25: Major Allied raids begin on Hamburg.
**AUG** 17: USAAF raid Schweinfurt and Regensburg; RAF bomb the V1 and V2 station at Peenemunde.
**SEP**  8: Italian surrender announced.
10: German troops occupy Rome.
29: Italy signs full armistice terms.
**OCT** 13: Italy declares war on Germany.
**NOV** 22: RAF attack opens "the Battle of Berlin."
28: The Tehran Conference takes place.
**DEC** 24: Eisenhower named Supreme Allied Commander for the "Second Front."

## 1944
**JAN** 22: Allies land at Anzio.
27: Lifting of blockade of Leningrad by Red Army.
**MAR**  4: The USAAF begin daylight raids on Berlin.
19: German troops occupy Hungary.
**JUN**  4: Rome falls to the Allies.
6: D-Day: the Western Allies land in Normandy.
13/14: First flying bombs (V1) are launched.
**JUL** 20: Bomb plot against Hitler.
**AUG**  1: Warsaw Uprising begins.
15: Allies land in the South of France.
23–25: Liberation of Paris.
25: Rumania declares war on Germany.
**SEP**  3: Brussels liberated.
5: Bulgaria declares war on Germany.
8: First V2 rocket lands in Chiswick, London.
12: US 1st Army enter Aachen.
17: Airborne landings at Arnhem.
**OCT**  3: Polish Home Army in Warsaw surrenders.
18: Conscription of all able-bodied German men aged between 16 and 60 for the *Volkssturm*.
24: US 1st Army capture Aachen.
**DEC** 16: The Ardennes Offensive launched.

## 1945
**JAN** 11: Ardennes offensive collapses.
12: Soviet offensive on the Eastern Front.
20: Hungary signs armistice with the United Nations.
26: Auschwitz liberated by the Red Army.
**FEB** 4–11: Yalta Conference.
12: Women called up to join the *Volkssturm*.
13–14: Dresden devastated by RAF and USAAF.
23: Turkey declares war on Germany.
**MAR**  7: Red Army enters Kolberg. US Army take the bridge at Remagen across the Rhine.
20: Hitler's last public appearance.
23–24: British cross the Rhine.
30: Danzig captured by the Red Army.
**APR**  2: *Werwolf* resistance movement is established.
12: Roosevelt dies.
13: Vienna captured by the Red Army. Buchenwald liberated by US 3rd Army.
15: British 2nd Army liberate Belsen.
23: Himmler asks Count Bernadotte to negotiate, on his behalf, a separate peace with the Allies.
24: US troops liberate Dachau.
25: Western Allies reject Himmler's offer.
25: Russian and American troops link up at Torgau.
28: Mussolini shot by Italian partisans.
30: Hitler and his wife commit suicide. Munich captured by US 7th Army.
**MAY**  2: Berlin surrenders to the Red Army. German armies in Italy make complete surrender.
4: All enemy forces in Holland, North West Germany and Denmark surrender. US 7th Army captures Berchtesgaden.
7: Unconditional surrender of Germany.
8: VE Day.
10: Red Army occupies Prague and liberates Theresienstadt.
11–12: German troops in the Aegean, capitulate.
21: Himmler arrested and commits suicide on 23 May.
23: Arrest of Doenitz and his "government."
**JUN** 25: United Nations Charter adopted in San Francisco.
**JUL**  1: Allies start garrisoning of Berlin.
16: Potsdam Conference begins.
**NOV** 20: The trial of major war criminals begins at Nuremberg.

# Index